**PRACTICE
MAKES
PERFECT**®

English
Vocabulary
Games

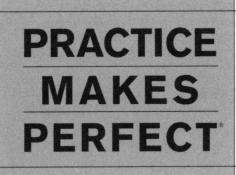

PRACTICE MAKES PERFECT®

English Vocabulary Games

Chris Gunn, Lanternfish ESL

Mc
Graw
Hill
Education

New York Chicago San Francisco Athens London Madrid
Mexico City Milan New Delhi Singapore Sydney Toronto

3   4   5   6   7   8   9   10   11   12   QVS/QVS   1   0   9   8   7   6   5

ISBN   978-0-07-182072-1
MHID   0-07-182072-8

Library of Congress Control Number 2013947031

McGraw-Hill Education, the McGraw-Hill Education logo, Practice Makes Perfect, and related trade dress are trademarks or registered trademarks of McGraw-Hill Education and/or its affiliates in the United States and other countries and may not be used without written permission. All other trademarks are the property of their respective owners. McGraw-Hill Education is not associated with any product or vendor mentioned in this book.

McGraw-Hill Education products are available at special quantity discounts to use as premiums and sales promotions or for use in corporate training programs. To contact a representative, please visit the Contact Us pages at www.mhprofessional.com.

This book is printed on acid-free paper.

Also by Chris Gunn
Easy ESL Crossword Puzzles

Contents

Introduction

This book contains a collection of vocabulary puzzles organized into 18 thematic units. Each unit is constructed around lists of important vocabulary words needed to discuss those themes. The lists range in difficulty from advanced beginner to intermediate, covering approximately 1,000 words. With this book, students can learn or review vocabulary items in a fun and motivating way. Teachers can supplement their lessons by introducing new vocabulary or providing games and puzzles for reviewing vocabulary taught in class.

Each unit begins with a *vocabulary workout*, which consists of a definition-matching activity. Other unit activities include identifying collocations (two words that appear together frequently) or sequencing vocabulary items. The vocabulary workout is meant to serve as a reference for the puzzles at the end of the unit, as many of the answers from the puzzles can be found somewhere in the vocabulary workout. As well, much of the vocabulary is utilized in more than one puzzle, which helps reinforce it. However, though there are links among the various puzzles, it is not necessary to use all of them at once.

Hints for solving the puzzles:

1. **Pay attention to collocations**. Roughly speaking, two words are collocations if they occur together frequently so that the combination of words seems natural, whereas combinations of similar words would seem awkward. For example, you *make friends*, but you usually do not say that you *make girlfriends*. In other words, *make* collocates with the word *friend* but not with the word *girlfriend*. Paying attention to which words collocate will help you supply answers to puzzles or at least eliminate some potential answers. To illustrate this point, consider the following clue:

   He was _____ with theft.

   The words *accused*, *blamed*, *charged*, *convicted*, *punished*, and *sentenced* are all potential candidates for answers in that they are all crime-related past participles of verbs. However, of that list of verbs, only *charged* collocates with *with*: People can be *charged* **with** a crime, whereas they are *accused* **of** a crime, *blamed* **for** a crime, *convicted* **of** a crime, *punished* **for** a crime, and *sentenced* **for** a crime. Thus, all of the words in the list can be eliminated except *charged*.

2. **Look for instances of word play**. Many fixed expressions in English become fixed expressions precisely because they contain word plays such as alliteration or rhyme. Alliteration is a repetition of sounds (often at the

beginning of words). On the other hand, two words rhyme if they have the same sound from the final stressed syllable to the end of the word. The proverb *practice makes perfect* and the idiom *burst your bubble* both contain alliteration. The proverb *haste makes waste* and the idiom *wear and tear* are examples of rhyme.

3. **Use a pencil**. Just because a word fits a particular blank doesn't mean it is the answer. You have to find a word that will solve the puzzle as a whole. If you are having trouble, go back and review the vocabulary workout. As a last resort, the answers to the puzzles are provided in the back of the book.

4. **Most of all, have fun!** These puzzles are meant to be an entertaining source of vocabulary review.

Movies

VOCABULARY

acting	comedy	historical drama	romantic comedy
action	costumes	horror	scenes
adventure	crime	mood	science fiction
animation	dialogue	mystery	script
character	documentary	plot	setting
cinematography	family	road movie	special effects
climax	fantasy	romance	thriller

PUZZLE 1·1

Definition match up: Movies, part 1 *Match the following definitions with the vocabulary words.*

1. The written copy of a movie _____

2. What the characters say _____

3. Movies about magic _____

4. Movies anyone can see _____

5. A movie about aliens or robots _____

6. What happens in a movie _____

7. A movie about a bank robbery _____

8. A movie that makes you laugh _____

9. Explosions and computer graphics _____

10. A movie about the past _____

11. A movie about real events _____

12. What movies are broken up into _____

13. The exciting finish _____

14. The time and place of a movie _____

15. Movies that frighten you _____

16. What the characters wear _____

17. A movie about solving a murder _____

18. A movie made by drawing or use of computer graphics _____

Genre or element? *The type of movie is called the movie* genre. *An* element *of a movie is one aspect of a movie that we can talk about. Sort the vocabulary words from the beginning of the chapter into the following categories.*

1. Movie genres _____

_____

_____

2. Elements of a movie _____

_____

_____

What does the critic think? *A* critic *is someone who watches a movie and decides if it is good or bad. If critics like a movie, they give it a* thumbs-up. *If they don't like a movie, they give it a* thumbs-down. *A* mixed review *is a review that has both good and bad things to say about the movie. Read the following reviews and decide if the critic is giving a* thumbs-up, *a* thumbs-down, *or a* mixed review.

1. "The cinematography was breathtaking." _____

2. "The plot was predictable and the script lacked originality." _____

3. "It was hilarious. I nearly bust a gut laughing so hard." _____

4. "The acting was convincing." _____

5. "The dialogue was cheesy, though the special effects were stunning." _____

_____

6. "It had a heart-warming story." _____

7. "It kept me on the edge of my seat." _____

8. "I wanted to leave about half-way through." _____

PUZZLE 1·4

Fill in the blanks *Complete the following paragraphs by filling in the blanks using the words provided.*

People in movies

actors   cameo   extras   role   starring   stunt   supporting   voices

People who perform in movies are called _____. A main actor, or a star,

is a person who has a lead _____, and we say that the movie

is _____ that actor. Many famous actors also supply the _____

for characters in animations. A _____ role is a part that is not as important

as the lead. A _____ is a short appearance in a film by a famous

actor. _____ are people who are in the background and who usually do not

have any dialogue. _____ performers are people who act in dangerous

scenes instead of actors.

Characters

antagonist   antihero   characters   costume   dialogue   main   protagonist   villain

The roles that actors play are called _____. What the characters say is called

the _____ and what a character wears is called the _____.

The _____ of a film is the _____ character, often referred to

as the hero. Not all main characters are heroic: A protagonist that lacks heroic qualities is called

an _____. The _____ is the character that comes into

conflict with the main character. An antagonist is often referred to as

the _____.

Setting and scenes

future   horror   mood   place   scene   set   take   time

The setting of a movie tells us the _____ and _____ of the

story. For example, historical dramas are _____ in the past, and many science

fiction movies _____ place in the _____. The setting of a

movie also helps to create _____. A dark, stormy setting might be used for a _____ film. Most movies have more than one setting. Often the setting changes with each _____.

Plot

car   formulaic   plot   sequence   synopsis   twist

What happens in a movie is called the _____. A short summary of the plot is called a _____. Some movies are _____, which means you can predict what is going to happen. For example, in many action films you know there is going to be a _____ chase and a fight _____. Still other movies surprise you with a plot _____, which is a sudden, unexpected change in the progression of the story.

Critics

mixed   pan   rave   reviews   thumbs-down   thumbs-up

Critics are people who watch movies and write _____. If critics really like a movie, they might write a _____ review. You can also say they give the movie a _____ if they write good things. On the other hand, they might _____ a movie if they don't like it. In this case, we say they gave it a _____. If critics have both good and bad things to say, we say the movie got _____ reviews.

PUZZLE 1·5

Word paths *Find and circle the secret words below by following a connected path through the maze. Some words may overlap. Then use the remaining letters to uncover a hidden message (a movie phrase):*

A	V	E	Q	U	E	L	A	C	A	S
R		S		B		O		X		T
G	O	Y	N	O	D	I	A	L	I	R
N		F		P		F		O		S
I	T	T	E	E	S	I	S	G	Y	C
T		C		E		C		U		E
W	I	S	S	P	I	R	U	E	C	N
C		T		T		C		E		E
A	S	R	O	M	R	O	S	T	U	M
N		E		A		L		U		
T	I	H	S	N	C	E	T	N		

1. Part II of a movie. __ __ __ __ __ __

2. One short segment of a movie. __ __ __ __ __

3. A sudden change in the plot. __ __ __ __ __

4. A protagonist who lacks heroic qualities. __ __ __ __ __ __ __ __

5. What a character wears. __ __ __ __ __ __ __

6. A movie in three parts. __ __ __ __ __ __ __ __

7. The written form of a movie. __ __ __ __ __ __

8. What the actors say. __ __ __ __ __ __ __ __

9. The group of actors in a movie. __ __ __ __

10. A movie about love. __ __ __ __ __ __ __

11. A summary of the plot. __ __ __ __ __ __ __ __

12. The part an actor plays. __ __ __ __

13. A dangerous piece of acting. __ __ __ __ __

14. A word used to describe a good review. __ __ __ __

15. The time and place of a story. __ __ __ __ __ __ __

Hidden message: Movie phrase: *What do you call a movie that does well?*

__ __ __ __ __   __ __ __ __ __ __ __   __ __ __ __ __ __

Riddles: Name that movie *Read the following movie descriptions and guess which movie is being discussed.*

1. It is a sci-fi blockbuster that takes place on an alien world. It's about the conflict that arises when humans try to mine resources on the alien planet. The native inhabitants are portrayed as large, athletic sentient beings who have great respect for the environment.

   Movie title: _____

2. It's a musical drama based on a novel by Victor Hugo. The main character Jean Valjean is a fugitive, running from police inspector Javert, played by Russell Crowe.

   Movie title: _____

3. It's an epic fantasy trilogy about an evil ring of power. The protagonist sets off on a quest to destroy the ring but must confront many enemies along the way, including himself.

   Movie title: _____

4. It's an animation about a little boy named Andy whose toys come to life when he leaves the room. It stars the voices of Tom Hanks and Tim Allen.

   Movie title: _____

5. It's an adventure story based on the best-selling novel by Yann Martel. It's about a young man who survives a shipwreck only to be trapped in a lifeboat with a tiger as the lifeboat drifts across the Pacific Ocean.

   Movie title: _____

6. It's a romance with a tragic ending. It's about a poor artist, played by Leonardo DiCaprio, who falls in love with an aristocrat's daughter while traveling across the Atlantic on a luxury cruise liner. In the end, the ship sinks and the artist gives up his life for his lover.

   Movie title: _____

7. It's a science fiction comedy that takes place on Earth. It's about a special team of agents who have to watch over the aliens living on Earth. Will Smith is in it.

   Movie title: _____

8. It's a science-fiction adventure directed by Steven Spielberg and based on a novel written by Michael Crichton. It's about a theme park for dinosaurs where things go horribly wrong.

   Movie title: _____

9. It's a psychological thriller starring Bruce Willis. He plays a child psychologist who counsels a boy who sees ghosts.

   Movie title: _____

Definition match up: Movies, part 2 *Match the following words to their definitions.*

actor	blockbuster	director	film crew	movie buff	subtitles	usher
audience	cast	extra	flop	role	synopsis	writer
B movie	critic	fan	mainstream	stunt performer	trailer	

1. The group of actors in a movie _____

2. The part an actor plays _____

3. A low-budget movie _____

4. An advertisement for a movie _____

5. The people who film the movie _____

6. A person who writes reviews _____

7. A summary of a movie plot _____

8. A highly successful movie _____

Matching: Movie collocations *Match the following words with their collocations (two words often used together).*

cameo	lead	rave	screen
car	movie	road	special
computer	plot	science	stunt

1. _____ adaptation

2. _____ graphics

3. _____ buff

4. _____ review

5. _____ twist

6. _____ appearance

7. _____ chase

8. _____ performer

9. _____ movie

10. _____ effects

11. _____ role

12. _____ fiction

Labeling: Movie vocabulary *Attach the label in the box to the following word lists.*

Equipment needed to make movies
Equipment needed to show movies
People who make movies
People who watch movies
Scenes from an action movie

Things heard in a movie
Words seen on movie screens
Words used to describe an actor's role
Words used to describe movie quality

1. _____

closing credits
opening credits
subtitles

2. _____

cast
film crew
stunt performers

3. _____

car chase
fight sequence
shoot out

4. _____

audience
critics
movie buffs

5. _____

camera
costumes
lights

6. _____

B movie
blockbuster
flop/bomb

7. _____

dialogue
sound effects
sound track

8. _____

lead/starring
minor
supporting

9. _____

projector
screen
speakers

Crossword *Fill in the correct word to solve the puzzle.*

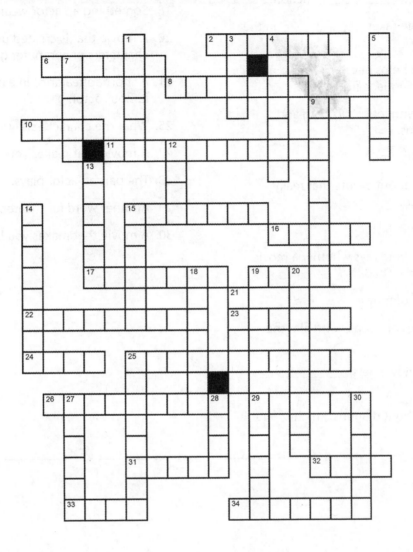

Across

2. Explosions, lights, and car crashes: _____ effects.

6. A bad movie gets _____ by the critics.

8. A place where people watch movies.

9. Another word for movie.

10. What happens in a movie.

11. A big, spectacular movie that costs millions of dollars to make.

15. The time and place of a movie.

16. The music in a movie: sound _____.

Down

1. Part II of a movie.

3. Actors _____ a part in a movie.

4. The text that tells you who helped to make the movie.

5. The exciting finish of a movie.

7. A person who acts in movies.

9. Completely predictable plot.

12. The group of actors in a movie.

13. What a movie is divided into.

14. A summary of a movie.

Across (cont.)

17. Movies about robots, spaceships, and the future: _____ fiction.

19. The movie takes _____ in the past.

22. Text that helps peop____ ____ ____ ___ and foreign language fi___

23. Movies with lots of fighting and explosions.

24. The main actor.

25. A movie about events that really happened.

26. A person in a story.

29. A person who says whether a movie was good or bad.

31. The type of movie.

32. The group of people who film the movie.

33. A good movie gets _____ reviews.

34. Movies about dragons, knights, and wizards.

Down (cont.)

15. The written form of the movie.

18. Something an actor wears.

20. A movie that is created using cartoon characters or computer graphics.

21. A short appearance in a movie by a famous actor.

25. What the characters say.

27. A movie that makes you afraid.

28. The part an actor plays.

29. Another word for theater.

30. A movie that makes you laugh.

Word search *Find the following words in the grid.*

```
F Z S S A N T A G O N I S T V T I Q M Q L N
A T M C B S C E N E P R O T A G O N I S T G
N D I R E C T O R S O U N D T R A C K W R O
T U L I S S O S P E C I A L E F F E C T S U
A Z S P A G S S F X H G T N O T V N S K R U
S C R T T H E A T E R D O E P K O F P E V I
Y E U P A Z U V L U M M M L Y I U S T U N T
I L D Y W R Y G T Z M A E K T O C C E K B S
L E U O R E V I E W C E Y C R V A U B A R O
H B L O C K B U S T E R A I F R G C B O V A
B R P P C U C O M E D Y X T A O O B T J Z A
C I U W R P M Y W Y T G C H L W U C Y O J N
C T H R I L L E R M S T C A D V E N T U R E
I Y C B T A X O N T I T I B C J F V A G D S
N V T J I W C A T T H D E N O M T I X N Q U
E Z E Y C L I M A X A Z M R G O P F L O J W
M Z Q R O M A N C E R R P O Y W U B O M V U
A F J A N I M A T I O N Y R O O F A M I L Y
```

Action	Cinema	Fantasy	Script
Actors	Climax	Film	Setting
Adventure	Comedy	Mystery	Sound track
Animation	Costume	Plot	Special effects
Antagonist	Critic	Projector	Star
Blockbuster	Dialogue	Protagonist	Stunt
Cameo	Director	Review	Theater
Celebrity	Documentary	Romance	Thriller
Character	Family	Scene	

Word jumble: Blockbuster *Find the words described below within the word "blockbuster." You can use the letters in any order, but you can only use each letter once.*

BLOCKBUSTER

HINT: USE THE CODE BREAKER TO THE RIGHT TO HELP YOU SOLVE THE WORDS.

CLUES	ANSWERS	CODE BREAKER
1. A color	_ _ _ _	1 2 x x
2. Another word for break	_ _ _ _	3 5 x 22
3. A place to hang clothes	_ _ _ _ _ _	6 2 x 7 x 8
4. Where you use a key	_ _ _ _ _	9 x 10 x
5. A sea animal with claws	_ _ _ _ _ _ _	11 x 3 13 x x 12
6. The outside of a loaf of bread	_ _ _ _ _	14 15 x 16 x
7. A baby bear	_ _ _	17 x 18
8. Something you see on an elephant	_ _ _ _	8 x 19 20
9. Another word for fortune	_ _ _ _	9 21 x x
10. A vehicle used to carry goods	_ _ _ _ _	22 x x 6 23
11. A vehicle for space travel	_ _ _ _ _ _	24 x 27 x x 25
12. An underwater vehicle	_ _ _	19 5 28
13. The past tense of break	_ _ _ _ _	x 12 x 23 x
14. The opposite of win	_ _ _ _	26 x 7 x
15. Yours and mine	_ _ _ _	x 5 24 19
16. Something to hold up pants	_ _ _ _ _	1 x 11 x
17. A square in 3-D	_ _ _ _ _	10 x 28 x
18. Another word for heal	_ _ _ _ _	17 x 29 x
19. The points in a game	_ _ _ _ _	13 27 x x x
20. The part an actor plays	_ _ _ _	29 x 9 x
21. The opposite of open	_ _ _ _ _	x 26 x 16 x
22. Another word for problem	_ _ _ _ _ _	22 x x x 18 2 x
23. Another word for steal	_ _ _	15 28
24. Clean something really hard	_ _ _ _ _	30 14 x 21 x
25. The past tense of strike	_ _ _ _ _	30 25 x x x 20

Television and entertainment

VOCABULARY

agent	game show	privacy
cartoon	gossip/rumors	public eye
celebrity/star	host	ratings
commercials	infomercial	reality TV
drama	late night TV	rerun
entertainer	laugh track	series
episode	makeover	sitcom
exposure	newscast	soap opera
fame	paparazzi	talent
fan	perform	talk show
footage	prime time	viewer

PUZZLE 2·1

Word list: Television and entertainment *The words in the vocabulary box are related to TV and entertainment. Look up any of the words you don't know and then find a word that could match each definition to the right. More than one word can fit some of the blanks.*

1. A famous person _____

2. Someone who gets jobs for actors _____

3. Someone who watches a show _____

4. Advertisements between programming _____

5. A television program that promotes a product for sale _____

6. A person who likes a celebrity _____

7. Stories about someone that may or may not be true _____

   _____

8. A show where a host interviews celebrities _____

9. A show where ordinary people compete against each other for prizes _____

   _____

13

10. A comedy program based on everyday life situations _____

_____

11. A serial daytime drama following the lives of various characters and their interactions

_____

12. A show in which someone is given new makeup, new clothes, and a new hairstyle _____

_____

13. An animated show (usually for children) _____

14. A show that provides information about world events _____

15. The time of day when the largest number of people are watching and the best TV programming is shown _____

16. People who stalk celebrities in order to take pictures _____

17. A person who talks to guests on a talk show _____

18. One show in a series or season _____

19. Being left alone and out of the public eye _____

20. A show that is being shown again _____

PUZZLE
2·2

Labeling: Television and entertainment *Attach television- and entertainment-related labels to the lists of words that follow.*

famous people   programming that advertises   shows that have hosts
people who watch shows   public renown   shows with multiple episodes

1. _____   4. _____

    game show   commercial
    talk show   infomercial

2. _____   5. _____

    celebrity   audience
    star   viewers

3. _____   6. _____

    fame   a season
    popularity   a mini-series

Fill in the blanks: Television and entertainment *Complete the paragraphs by filling in the blanks using the words provided.*

Prime time TV

advertising	evening	prime
consequence	networks	rush
drive	popular	viewers

_____ time is the time of day when the most people are watching TV.

Prime time is in the _____ after dinner when people relax after a hard day

at work. It is also the time of day when the television _____ earn most of

their _____ revenue. As a _____, it is also the time of day

when the networks air their most _____ shows. The more _____

a show has, the more money the network can charge advertisers. Prime time for radio is during

the morning and afternoon _____ hours when many people are in their cars

and thus is called _____ time.

Television programming

apartment	host	shows
contestants	newscasts	sitcoms
game	reality	talk

There are many different types of _____ on television. Some of the most

popular shows are _____, which are comedies about a group of

characters sharing a common environment such as an _____ or a

workplace. _____ shows, where a _____ interviews

celebrity guests, are also popular shows on TV. Many people enjoy _____

shows as well where _____ compete with each other to win prizes by

answering questions or doing challenges. In the last few decades, _____

shows, which often feature ordinary people doing unscripted actions, have gained a lot of

popularity. Finally, many people watch _____ to find out what's going on in

the world.

Advertising

advertising	benefits	placement
background	commercials	public
bathroom	infomercials	volume

With the exception of _____ television, which gets its funding from

government tax dollars, most television networks generate revenue

through _____. The most visible forms of advertisements

are _____, which are shown between segments of television programming. Commercials are not always as effective as advertisers would like since people turn down the _____ or use the time to run to the _____ or get snacks. And so, some advertisers also use product _____, in which the actors are seen using a product during the show or the product is seen in the _____. Finally, some advertisers even create whole shows called _____, which are dedicated to explaining the _____ of a certain product.

The paparazzi

camera	fascinated	privacy
crime	paparazzi	relationship
fans	photo	scandal

Celebrities generate a tremendous amount of interest among their _____. In short, the public is _____ by celebrity lives. And so, there is a whole industry devoted to catching celebrities on _____. The public wants to know what celebrities are doing and who they are in a _____ with. If a celebrity commits a _____ or is involved in a _____, it's big news. The people who follow celebrities and take their pictures are called _____. They can make big money if they can catch a celebrity in a compromising _____. Of course, celebrities complain that they have a right to _____ and that this is a violation of that right.

Crossword

Across

1. People who follow celebrities and take pictures of them.

3. A show where contestants compete for prizes. (4, 4)

5. Taking pictures of celebrities in their homes (when they don't want to): An invasion of _____.

6. A comedy where a cast of characters shares an environment such as a house or workplace.

8. Ordinary people in general: The _____.

12. A person who really likes a show or celebrity.

Down

2. A measure of how popular shows are.

3. Stories about someone that may or may not be true.

4. A show where celebrities get interviewed by a host. (4, 4)

7. A show where people have their clothes, hair, or makeup completely changed and a comparison is made between before and after.

9. A person who competes in game shows.

10. An advertisement that is shown between segments of a TV show.

11. A person who watches a show.

13. A show where people learn what's happening in the world.

15. The focus of public attention: In the public _____.

17. A show that has already been broadcast before.

18. Act, sing, or play a musical instrument in a show.

19. A type of advertising in which actors use products during a show: Product _____.

21. The group of people who watch a show.

24. A show that usually has regular people doing unscripted actions. (7, 4)

25. A person who is interviewed on a talk show.

26. A television program with many episodes.

27. A place where shows are filmed.

28. An animated show for children.

12. Another word for renown.

14. A daytime drama that follows the lives of many different characters and their interactions. (4, 5)

16. The time of day when the most people are watching TV. (5, 4)

20. A popular TV personality.

22. One part of a TV series.

23. The person who interviews guests on a talk show.

Word search: Television and entertainment *Find the words below in the grid.*

```
N H F E N T E R T A I N E R P Z E J D M U Z I K
S C O O T J S L U Y I E C K Y G A B H R N M L O
Q E G S B F O N E B L W F S E G M E N T N M G M
E L A T T D A M R E A S A T A L K S H O W G I G
Q E M U C K P S I G U A M T Y X S P O P R Z B N
P B E E N X S T H U G N E A Z S P T M A Z B C S
R R S D B D P A Q Y H C O M M E R C I A L M Z W
I I H Z P R O R T N H H B U A P E R F O R M S
V T O U R A T I V E R O E X C M N A Z N D X G P
A Y W S I M L Y I T A R X A L M P F X S U N V W
C D R R M A I Z E W C R E P F A E S E R I E S R
Y G E F E S G V W O K A I R P S T S I T C O M W
W N P R T H H V E R O S B Y U J N E A J N Z S F
L S I F I Y T Y R K S E A L R N W R N W T O S V
F A S C M P W A M O D E L O E P U B L I C E Y E
R Z O V E E D A G E N T M O Z B G Y N P G J R B
R X D M A K E O V E R U N E W S C A S T J H N A
M T E X T A L E N T R A T U J F F W O C P T T P
```

Agent	Game show	Newscast	Segment
Cable	Gossip	Paparazzi	Series
Cartoon	Host	Perform	Sitcom
Celebrity	Hype	Prime time	Soap
Commercial	Late night	Privacy	Spotlight
Drama	Laugh track	Public eye	Star
Entertainer	Makeover	Ratings	Talent
Episode	Model	Reality	Talk show
Fame	Network	Rerun	Viewer
Fan	News anchor	Rumor	

Word paths: Television and entertainment *Find and circle the secret words below by following a connected path through the maze. Some words may overlap. Then use the remaining letters to uncover an idiom related to celebrity status.*

C	E	L	E	B	M	O	D	E	P	I
O	■	Y	■	R	■	O	■	L	■	S
N	T	E	U	I	T	Y	R	E	D	O
T	■	S	■	C	■	L	■	A	■	A
N	A	T	I	L	A	E	M	M	O	C
I	■	Y	■	M	R	■	T	■	T	
P	E	R	N	A	T	C	I	A	L	K
C	■	F	■	F	O	■	F	■	S	
A	A	O	R	M	E	T	M	W	O	H
R	■	N	■	I	■	I	■	E	■	S
T	O	O	P	R	E	M	O	C	T	I

1. One show in a series. __ __ __ __ __ __ __

2. Somebody you see on a game show. __ __ __ __ __ __ __ __ __ __ __

3. A person who displays new fashions. __ __ __ __ __

4. A show where famous people are interviewed. __ __ __ __ __ __ __ __ __

5. A children's animation. __ __ __ __ __ __ __

6. When many people watch TV. __ __ __ __ __ __ __ __ __

7. A TV advertisement. __ __ __ __ __ __ __ __ __

8. A show that is unscripted. __ __ __ __ __ __ __

9. Sing, dance, or play an instrument on TV. __ __ __ __ __ __ __

10. A person who adores a celebrity. __ __ __

11. A famous person. __ __ __ __ __ __ __ __ __

12. Short for situation comedy. __ __ __ __ __ __

13. Play a part in a TV drama. __ __ __ __

Hidden message: A celebrity-related idiom: *What you are well known for:*

__ __ __ __   __ __ __ __ __   __ __   __ __ __ __

Food and cooking

VOCABULARY

Food and cooking verbs

add	drain	pare	smoke
bake	fry	peel	steam
baste	grate	pickle	stir
boil	grease	pour	strain
chop	grill	preheat	whip
cube	marinate	roast	
deep fry	microwave	simmer	
dice	mix	slice	

PUZZLE
3·1

Definition match up: Cooking verbs *The vocabulary words in the box above are all cooking-related verbs. Look up any verbs you don't know. Next, find a word that could match each definition. More than one answer is possible.*

1. Combine ingredients together. _____

2. Soak meat in liquid containing spices. _____

3. Add oil to a pan so that food won't stick to it. _____

4. Take the skin off of a fruit or vegetable. _____

5. Cook something by submerging it in boiling oil. _____

6. Cut into small cubes. _____

7. Cook bread or cake in an oven. _____

8. Cook something in very hot (bubbling) water. _____

9. Cook something just below boiling. _____

10. Get the oven temperature ready before you cook. _____

11. Get rid of a liquid from something. _____

12. Put a liquid into something. _____

13. Cook a turkey or a chicken in an oven. _____

14. Cook using heated moisture. _____

15. Cook something in a pan on the stove. _____

16. Cook something over an open fire. _____

17. Cook something using smoke from a fire. _____

PUZZLE
3·2

Labeling: Cooking expressions *Attach the food- and cooking-related labels to the following lists of words.*

condiments	cooking utensils	shellfish
cooking apparel	dairy products	spices
cooking appliances	fruits and vegetables	types of meat

1. _____

   oven/stove/blender/microwave

2. _____

   chef's hat/apron/oven mitts

3. _____

   oregano/basil/chili pepper/rosemary

4. _____

   mustard/ketchup/soy sauce/relish

5. _____

   cabbage/lettuce/pineapple/plum

6. _____

   spatula/soup ladle/measuring cup

7. _____

   beef/pork/poultry/fish

8. _____

   oysters/clams/crabs/shrimp

9. _____

   cheese/milk/yogurt/cream

Matching: Amounts and containers collocations *Match the words in the box with their collocations below.*

a bottle   a bowl   a clove   a cup   a dash   a head   a jar   a loaf

1. _____ of garlic   5. _____ of ketchup

2. _____ of soup   6. _____ of lettuce

3. _____ of bread   7. _____ of salt

4. _____ of coffee   8. _____ of jam

Fill in the blanks: Food and cooking *Complete the paragraphs by filling in the blanks using the words provided.*

Cooking utensils

flip	pan	spatula
ladle	pot	strainer
measuring	recipes	utensils

Before you start cooking, you have to make sure you have the right cooking

_____ for the job. If you are going to boil something on the stove, you will

need a _____. If you are going to fry something, you will need

a _____. If you are going to _____ something over like a

burger or an egg, you will need a _____. If you are going to serve soup, you

will need a _____. If you are going to drain water from noodles, you will need

a _____. You will also need a _____ cup so that you are

able to add the amounts of ingredients that the _____ require.

Food preparation

chop	cutting	ingredients	mitts
counter	handling	meal	shopping

When you are preparing a _____, you should make sure you have all of

the _____ that the recipe requires. If not, you may have to make

a _____ list and go to the store. You will also need space to work.

Most kitchens have _____ space where you can prepare food. If you are

going to _____ vegetables, you should use a _____ board

to protect the counter. Before _____ the food, you should wash your hands thoroughly with soap and water. If you are going to be handling hot food, you may need some oven _____.

Making bread

bake cover flour knead loaf mix preheat rise

To make the dough, _____ one cup of _____ with salt, oil, and yeast in a bowl. Next, _____ the dough on a lightly floured surface until smooth. Place in a bowl and _____ with a damp cloth. Allow the dough to _____ for about an hour. When the dough has risen, place it into a _____ pan. _____ the oven to 350 degrees F (175 degrees C). Finally, _____ the dough in the oven for about 30 minutes.

Making pizza

crust   oven   spread
grate   pepperoni   sprinkle
grease   rolling   toppings

First, _____ your baking pan so that the dough will not stick to the pan.

Next, using a _____ pin, flatten the dough and spread it onto the pan.

Then, _____ tomato sauce evenly over the dough. _____ some mozzarella cheese and _____ it onto the sauce. Add other _____ such as mushrooms, _____, ham, or pineapple as desired. Preheat the _____. Finally, place the pizza in the oven and let bake until the _____ is a golden brown.

Making chili

diced drain ladle meat serve shredded simmer stirring

Place _____ in a large pot and brown. _____ off excess grease. Next, add chili beans, _____ tomatoes, onions, celery, and spices to the pot. Let the chili _____ on low heat for two hours, _____ occasionally. Use a _____ to pour chili into bowls. _____ with corn chips and _____ cheese.

Word search: Cooking *Find the following words in the grid.*

```
M E A S U R I N G C U P X U Y D S E A F O O D C
V W R D T N I Z D F G I A Q A V Z C M K Y J Q R
E K X I D O E H F P M R K L A W W V T R C K W O
Q Q K Q U F V P S E A V A E U Y Z S I K O C K Z
J H D D A I S E R O A S T T T F M A P O D N M P
G S P Y U R C H O P N U T W E T D A B A I Q G I
W A P O U L T R Y K B C F A Y B L K R A T R Z B
W A B I N G R E D I E N T S P Q O E R I C U I R
W P K Y C Q P O T S Y F P T A O K T Z X N Z L D
N R D N S E Y A E I E Y O I C A S O Q K Z A M A
U O J J H R E L L L Q I R R B Z Q S L I C E T B
T N O R F Y B I D K W X K A R M I C R O W A V E
E H I T I A O A J O V E N S I M M E R C M M N Z
N H J K T B L H N G R I L L U U D A M M B H V Y
S A G E P X U A H F P I D G P U F W C R D J Y V
I M G T P E P T L U K E I B E E F U E N G A C B
L E J T O R L I S O V G C F E L B H I G M E C G
V A O L V Q X X W V T I E B L R E C I P E T N L
```

Apron	Grill	Pan	Simmer
Bake	Herb	Pasta	Slice
Beef	Ingredients	Peel	Spatula
Boil	Kettle	Pork	Spice
Chop	Ladle	Pot	Stir
Cookbook	Marinate	Poultry	Stove
Dairy	Measuring cup	Recipe	Strain
Dice	Microwave	Roast	Utensil
Fry	Mix	Salad	Vegetables
Grate	Oven	Seafood	Wok

Crossword

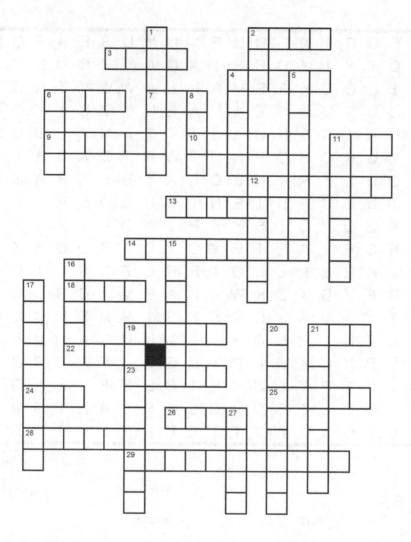

Across

2. Take the skin off of a potato or apple.

3. Heat water until it bubbles over.

4. Where you cook things.

6. Meat that comes from cows.

7. Something coffee is served in.

9. An appliance used to boil water for tea.

10. A list of directions for making food.

11. What you fry things in.

Down

1. A place where people cook.

2. What you boil things in.

4. Something added to food to give it flavor.

5. An onion, carrot, or cucumber.

6. _____ a cake or cookies in an oven.

8. Meat that comes from pigs.

11. Meat that comes from chickens or other birds.

Across (cont.)

12. Use a _____ to flip the burgers.

13. _____ a chicken in the oven.

14. An appliance that is used to heat food quickly.

18. Where you bake things.

19. Use oven _____ to carry a hot dish.

21. Combine ingredients.

22. _____ some tomatoes into small cubes.

23. Something cooks wear to keep their fronts clean.

24. _____ an egg in a pan.

25. Milk products like cheese and cream.

26. Something soup is served in.

28. _____ on low heat for two hours.

29. Things you use in your recipes.

Down (cont.)

12. _____ the water from noodles before you serve them.

15. A flat place in a kitchen where food is prepared.

16. Chop onions on a cutting _____.

17. Seafood that comes from animals like clams, oysters, crabs, and shrimp.

19. Use a _____ cup to add the correct amount of ingredients.

20. Mustard, ketchup, or relish.

21. Soak meat in a liquid with spices and herbs.

27. A utensil that is used to put soup into bowls.

Word paths: Cooking *Find and circle these secret words by following a connected path through the maze. Some words may overlap. Then use the remaining letters to uncover a hidden message: an idiom related to people.*

S	S	I	H	T	S	R	G	U	B	A
P	■	M	■	I	■	I	■	C	■	K
A	N	M	E	R	L	L	G	O	E	E
T	■	R	■	I	■	S	■	U	■	R
U	L	A	T	E	D	I	E	N	T	E
D	■	H	■	R	■	E	■	B	■	C
I	E	I	N	G	D	A	T	S	L	I
C	■	S	■	T	■	I	■	A	■	P
E	S	A	T	E	Y	R	R	O	A	E
M	■	N	■	U	■	C	■	E	■	E
A	R	I	M	I	C	R	O	W	A	V

1. Cook meat over an open flame. __ __ __ __ __

2. Directions for cooking something. __ __ __ __ __ __

3. Chop into small cubes. __ __ __ __ __

4. Mix a liquid with a spoon. __ __ __ __ __

5. Cook on low heat. __ __ __ __ __ __

6. A piece of pizza or a piece of cheese. __ __ __ __ __

7. A utensil used to flip burgers. __ __ __ __ __ __ __ __

8. Products made from milk. __ __ __ __ __

9. Something you use as part of a recipe. __ __ __ __ __ __ __ __ __ __

10. Cook a chicken in an oven. __ __ __ __ __

11. A flat space used to prepare food. __ __ __ __ __ __ __

12. An appliance used to heat food quickly. __ __ __ __ __ __ __ __ __

13. Soak meat in a sauce overnight. __ __ __ __ __ __ __ __

14. Cook a cake in an oven. __ __ __ __

Hidden message: Cooking proverb: *The secret to good cooking:*

__ __ __ __ __ __ __   __ __   __ __ __   __ __ __ __   __ __ __ __ __

PUZZLE 3·8

Idiom puzzle: Food idioms *Complete the following food-related idioms. Use the shape symbols below the blanks to help you solve the missing blanks. Each symbol represents one letter. Then use the numbers under the letters to solve the cooking proverb at the end.*

1. The best of the best:
THE _ _ _ _ _ _ OF THE CROP
♥ ♦ 24 ♠ 17

2. Something to think about:
_ _ _ _ _ FOR THOUGHT
2 ■ ■ 31

3. An extra benefit on an already good deal:
THE _ _ _ _ _ _ ON THE CAKE
★ ♥ 1

4. Identical:
LIKE TWO _ _ _ _ _ IN A POD
♣ ♠ 11

5. Incentives to do something:
THE _ _ _ _ _ _ _ AND THE STICK
♥ ♠ ♦ ♦ 18 ▼

6. Someone dear to you:
THE _ _ _ _ _ OF YOUR EYE
♠ ♣ ♣ 25 16

7. Get upset over something you can't change:
CRY OVER SPILT _ _ _ _ _
21 ★ 15 ◐

8. Rescue someone:
SAVE SOMEONE'S _ _ _ _ _ _
30 ♥ ■ 19

9. Very flat:
FLAT AS A _ _ _ _ _ _ _ _
♣ 22 ♥ ♠ ◐ 10

10. Simple to do:
EASY AS _ _ _ _
♣ 4

11. A hard problem to solve:
A TOUGH _ _ _ _ TO CRACK
14 ▼

12. Doesn't meet your standards:
DOESN'T CUT THE _ _ _ _ _ _ _ _
27 ⊡ 20 ▼ ♠ ♦ ▲

13. In a bad situation:
IN A _ _ _ _ _ _
♣ 8 ♥ 23 32

14. A person who sits and watches TV all day:
A COUCH _ _ _ _ _ _ _
♣ 28 ▼ ♠ ▼ 13

15. An easy way to make money quickly:
THE _ _ _ _ _ _ TRAIN
7 ♦ ♠ 9

16. Very different:
LIKE CHALK AND _ _ _ _ _ _ _
♥ 6 26

17. Be skeptical about something:
TAKE WITH A GRAIN OF _ _ _ _ _
♠ 3 ▼

18. An easy thing to do:
TAKING _ _ _ _ _ _ FROM A BABY
♥ ♠ 29 ▲ 12

19. Something you are not allowed to do:
FORBIDDEN _ _ _ _ _ _
5 ♦ ⊡ ★ ▼

Code breaker: a proverb related to food: *Make the best out of a bad situation:*

_ _   _ _ _ _   _ _ _ _ _   _ _ _   _ _ _ _ _ _ ,   _ _ _ _
1 2   3 4 5 6   7 8 9 10 11   12 13 14   15 16 17 18 19 20   21 22 23 24

_ _ _ _ _ _ _ _
25 26 27 28 29 30 31 32

Food and cooking **29**

City life and country life

City life

VOCABULARY			
airport	convenience store	intersection	restaurant
alley	crosswalk	library	shopping mall
apartment	factory	museum	sidewalk
bakery	fire department	office building	stadium
bank	gallery	parking lot	subway station
café/coffee shop	gas station	pharmacy	supermarket
cinema/movie theater	hospital	police station	university
clinic	hotel	post office	warehouse

PUZZLE 4·1

Definition match up: Cities *Match the following definitions with the vocabulary words.*

1. A place where people save money _____

2. A place to borrow books _____

3. A place to buy fuel _____

4. A place to safely cross a road _____

5. A place to hold art exhibitions _____

6. A place to order food _____

7. A place to exhibit artifacts _____

8. A place where many people live _____

9. A place to walk next to a road _____

10. A place to mail a parcel _____

11. A place to board airplanes _____

12. A place to buy medicine _____

13. A place to see sporting events _____

14. A place where two roads meet _____

15. A small road between buildings _____

16. A place where surgery is performed _____

17. A place to store goods _____

18. A place to put vehicles _____

Label the word lists: About a city *Choose one of the following phrases to label the word lists.*

areas of a city   entertainment venues   public transportation
cultural facilities   housing   retail vendors
educational facilities   medical facilities   transport infrastructure

1. _____

apartment
house
townhouse

2. _____

bus
subway
train

3. _____

gallery
library
museum

4. _____

clinic
doctor's office
hospital

5. _____

bridges
parking lots
roads

6. _____

movie theater
nightclub
sports staduim

7. _____

downtown/city center
suburb
neighborhood

8. _____

college
school
university

9. _____

convenience store
department store
shopping mall

Word search: Places in a city *Find these words in the grid.*

```
C P S F I R E D E P A R T M E N T N I P K T
T O U Y L I F E I Y S M I L K Y O L O L N C
I L B U N I V E R S I T Y N C I O T A E I N
S I W O F P E A O P L E A A T T S W M N B M
E C A I N B R I D G E B M C R S S T I G U L
S E Y O N B K E L S O R E O U S R L M I E T
K S S O I C G O E T A S P B O A C T D H E R
Y T T L O S O T N H R R H R P I S A C I T Y
S A A D I H H A P E I S C A W Y T H A T I T
C T T B C I R O T A L L E Y R S S B E C A U
R I I S A U S N P T S U P E R M A R K E T E
A O O I A K I P T E S C L S I D E W A L K I
P N N T E T E A I R C L G A S S T A T I O N
E R S R Z E N R S A A A R E B U I L D I N G
R E O W H A T K Y G T H F W A R E H O U S E
R T E A C O U R T H O U S E Y F A C T O R Y
S A R E D Q Q V D B F H P O S T O F F I C E
```

Airport	Clinic	Library	Sidewalk
Alley	Courthouse	Park	Skyscraper
Apartment	Crosswalk	Pharmacy	Stadium
Bakery	Dock	Police station	Store
Bank	Factory	Post office	Subway station
Bridge	Fire department	Restaurant	Supermarket
Building	Gallery	Road	Theater
Bus stop	Gas station	School	University
Café	Intersection	Shop	Warehouse

Hidden messages: City life *Once you have found all of the words in the word search (puzzle 4·3), look at the remaining (uncircled) letters to find two hidden messages. Uncover the messages and fill in the blanks.*

Quotation 1: _ _ _ _ _   _ _ _ _ _   _ _   _ _ _ _ _ _ _ _   _ _

_ _ _ _ _   _ _ _ _   _ _ _ _ _ _ _   _ _ _ _ _ _ _ _

— Henry David Thoreau

Quotation 2: _ _ _ _ _   _ _ _ _ _   _ _   _ _ _ _ _   _ _

_ _ _ _ _ _ _   _ _ _ _ _ _   _ _ _ _ _ _ _   _ _ _ _

_ _ _ _   _ _ _ _ _

—Plato

Crossword

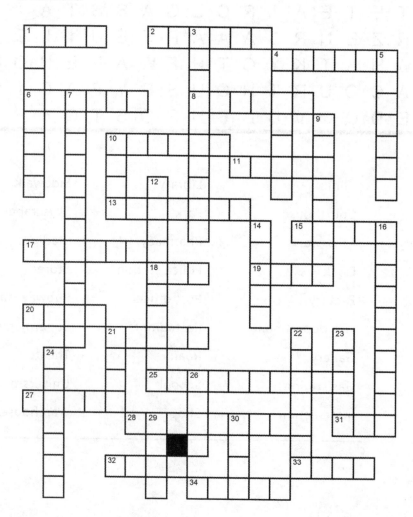

Across

1. A place where people live.

2. A place where you see historical artifacts.

4. A place where children learn.

6. A place where criminals are kept.

8. A train that goes underground.

10. A place outside a city where many people live and commute to the city.

11. A large group of people.

13. A place where people display works of art.

15. The leader of a city.

17. A place where people make things.

18. A place where people work out.

19. A place where people save money.

20. A place where people wait for the bus: A bus _____.

21. A place where criminals are put on trial.

25. A place where people can buy a variety of goods: A _____ store.

27. An activity that is against the law.

28. A place where many families live together in the same building.

31. A place where people park their cars: A parking _____.

32. A time when many people commute: _____ hour.

33. A place where people drive cars.

34. A small road between buildings.

Down

1. A place where sick people are treated.

3. A very tall building.

4. A place where people board trains, subways, and intercity buses.

5. A place where people borrow books.

7. A place where two roads meet.

9. A place next to a road where people walk.

10. Air pollution.

12. A place where children play.

14. A word meaning city: the opposite of rural.

16. A place where people order food.

21. A place where people drink coffee.

22. A place where people see movies.

23. A place where people from out of town sleep.

24. A place where people board airplanes.

26. A place where people can go for walks.

29. A place where people mail parcels and letters: A _____ office.

30. A place where many shops are gathered under one roof: A shopping _____.

Fill in the blanks: City life *Complete the following paragraphs by filling in the blanks using the words provided.*

Facilities

advantage   clinics   college   library   medical   park   public

One _____ of living in a large city is that there are many facilities to serve you. When you are sick, you can visit _____ facilities such as _____ or hospitals. If you are passionate about learning, you can attend a community _____ or a university. If you need to do some research, you can go to a local _____ and check out a book. And if you just want to relax, you can head down to a _____ and spend the day watching people. And wherever you need to go, you can usually hop on _____ transportation to get you there.

Culture and entertainment

dancing   gallery   nightlife   stadium
friends   history   restaurant   theater

Another advantage of living in a large city is there is a lot to do. If you are bored, you can go to a _____ and see a movie. If you are hungry, you can go to a _____ and order food. If you enjoy watching sports, you can head down to the local _____ and get tickets for a game. If you are into art, you can visit a _____ and if you are interested in _____ you can visit a museum. If you are looking for some _____ you can go _____ at a club or meet _____ at a café.

City traffic

bumper   commuting   congestion   honking   park   rush   standstill

One problem with living in a city is traffic _____, especially when everyone is _____ to and from work. During _____ hour, traffic can be _____ to bumper and come to a _____. During traffic jams, people get angry and start _____ their horns. And to make matters worse, when you do get to your destination, there is often no place to _____ your car.

Pollution

drink   noise   problem   running   smog   waste

Another serious _____ with living in the city is the pollution. Car
exhaust causes a layer of air pollution called _____ to hover over the
city. _____ pollution is another issue with so many vehicles on the road;
people are _____ their engines and honking their horns. And finally, when
people put _____ down the drains and into the sewers, the water around a
city can become dirty and dangerous to _____ .

City infrastructure

bridges   crime   department   emergency   infrastructure   sewer   taxes   water

Cities require good _____ to run properly. Roads and _____
are needed to keep the traffic flowing. Clean _____ and electricity have to
be distributed to homes and businesses. A _____ system is needed to get rid
of wastewater. A police force is needed to keep _____ under control. And a
fire _____ has to be on duty at all times in case of _____ .
All of this infrastructure requires money, which is usually raised by
collecting _____ .

Collocation clues: City words *For each question, find one word that fits in all three blanks. Use those letters to solve the secret idiom code in puzzle 4·8.*

1. in _____ _____ transportation _____ office

   Answer: __ __ __ __ __
        25 22   29

2. _____ line _____ station _____ ticket

   Answer: __ __ __ __ __ __
       23 14

3. air _____ noise _____ water _____

   Answer: __ __ __ __ __ __ __ __
       21   15 30 11 32

4. police _____ train _____ gas _____

   Answer: __ __ __ __ __ __ __
       20 9 36 6 12

5. _____ light _____ accident _____ jam

   Answer: __ __ __ __ __ __ __
       5 19 35 1 8

6. _____ system _____ drain _____ pipe

   Answer: __ __ __ __ __ __
       4 2 13 27

7. _____ building head _____ post _____

   Answer: __ __ __ __ __ __
       31   26

8. _____ rate _____ of passion _____ and punishment

   Answer: __ __ __ __ __
       33   16 18

9. fire _____ _____ store _____ of defense

   Answer: __ __ __ __ __ __ __ __ __
       17 3 7 34 24   28

Three idioms. *Use the letters in puzzle 4·7 to complete the three idioms below.*

1. good times or bad: __ __ __ __ __   __ __   __ __ M __ __ __
                                  1 2 3 4 5   6 7   8 9   11 12 13

2. heavy traffic: __ __ __ __ __ __   __ __   __ __ __ __ __ __ __
                    14 15 16 17 18 19   20 21   22 23 24 25 26 27

3. revenge: __ __ __   __ __ __   __ __ __
             28 29 30   31 32 33   34 35 36

Sorting: City versus country *Cities and towns are* urban *areas. Places in the countryside are* rural *areas. Write* U *next to the words that are usually associated with urban areas and an* R *next to the words that are usually associated with rural areas. Then match the words with the definitions that follow.*

agriculture	factories	medical facilities	rush hour
boredom	farms	nightlife	scenery
cattle	fields	overcrowding	shopping malls
crime	fresh air	pollution	skyscrapers
crops	harvest	property value	smog
crowds	high cost of living	public transportation	starry skies
culture	high population	ranches	traffic
educational facilities	job opportunities	relaxation	unemployment
entertainment	livestock	resource industries	wildlife
excitement	manufacturing	retirement	woodlands

1. Animals raised by people _____

2. Another way to say cows _____

3. Forests _____

4. Very high buildings _____

5. Industries like mining and forestry _____

6. Farming and animal husbandry _____

7. Air pollution _____

8. Animals in nature _____

Country life

Fill in the blanks: Life in the country *Complete the following paragraphs by filling in the blanks using the words provided.*

Work in the country

agriculture   farmers   livestock   resource

crops   forestry   ranchers   rural

Many people who live in _____ areas work in _____, which is the growing of _____ and the raising of _____. People who grow crops are called _____ and people who raise animals like cattle or sheep are called _____. Other people who live in the country work in _____ industries such as mining and _____.

Country life

crime   fields   fresh   hustle   starry   traffic   wildlife

Many people move to the country to get away from the _____ and bustle of the big cities. They can relax in peace surrounded by forests and farmers' _____. If they are lucky, they can step outside their door and see abundant _____ such as deer and birds. They can enjoy the _____ air and the _____ skies at night. They can also avoid the heavy _____ and high _____ rate of the cities.

Exodus from the country

cost   education   nightlife   university

drawn   natural   opportunities   venues

In spite of all the _____ beauty of the country, many young people choose to move to cities. In some cases, they are following better job _____. In other cases, they are seeking to further their _____ by attending a college or a _____. Still others are _____ by the excitement of the cities where there is a lot to do. There are entertainment _____ such as theaters, galleries, and stadiums. There is also abundant _____ found at clubs, cafés, and restaurants. However, they are often surprised by the high _____ of living and the difficulty in finding decent housing.

Rhyming riddles: Things people do in the country *Find a word that solves the rhyming riddles below.*

1. Something ranchers raise that rhymes with battle? — — — — — —

2. Something ranchers raise that rhymes with deep? — — — — —

3. Something ranchers raise that rhymes with courses? — — — — — —

4. Something farmers grow that rhymes with horn? — — — —

5. Something farmers grow that rhymes with mice? — — — —

6. Something farmers grow that rhymes with beat? — — — —

7. Something farmers harvest that rhymes with mops? — — — — —

8. A place where crops grow that rhymes with yield? — — — — —

9. A farm vehicle that rhymes with factor? — — — — — — —

10. Something loggers chop that rhymes with bees? — — — — —

11. Something loggers use that rhymes with faxes? — — — — —

12. Something loggers use that rhymes with paws? — — — —

13. Something miners dig for that rhymes with door? — — —

14. A place where miners work that rhymes with dine? — — — —

Crossword

Across

2. Another way to say gather crops.

5. The season when farmers harvest their crops.

6. Rock with metal in it that miners dig for.

7. A person who raises cattle or sheep.

10. Something you catch in rivers, lakes, and streams.

12. A tool used to cut wood.

15. A black bird that steals the crops.

16. Something that farmers use to guard the crops.

Down

1. A person who works in underground mines.

2. An animal people ride.

3. Something farmers plant to grow crops.

4. A building on a farm used to keep animals.

5. A tool used to chop wood.

8. A crop that rhymes with horn.

9. Mining and forestry: _____ industries.

11. Animals raised by people.

Across (cont.)

18. The season when farmers plant their crops.

20. A crop often used in making bread.

21. A word that describes places in the country.

22. In the country, you can see _____ skies at night.

25. The raising of animals and growing of crops.

28. In the country, you can breathe _____ air.

30. Something farmers harvest.

31. A person who grows crops.

32. Many people move to the country when they _____.

Down (cont.)

13. A person who chops down trees.

14. A tool used to turn the soil (usually in the spring).

17. A small house in the country.

19. A system for bringing water to the crops.

20. Animals in the forest and mountains.

23. A crop that grows in paddies.

24. A vehicle used by farmers.

26. A bird that crows at the crack of dawn.

27. Another way to say cows.

29. Go for a walk up a mountain.

Word scramble: Harvest moon *Find the words described within the phrase "harvest moon." You can use the letters in any order, but you can only use each letter once.*

HARVEST MOON

HINT: USE THE CODE BREAKER TO THE RIGHT TO HELP YOU SOLVE THE WORDS.

CLUES	ANSWERS	CODE BREAKER
1. A brave person	_ _ _ _	1 x 2 x
2. The opposite of south	_ _ _ _ _	x 3 27 x x
3. The opposite of west	_ _ _ _	4 26 x x
4. A woman who raises a child	_ _ _ _ _ _	5 x 6 x x x
5. An animal with antlers	_ _ _ _ _	5 7 8 x x
6. A flower with thorns	_ _ _ _ _	9 10 x x
7. A king's chair	_ _ _ _ _ _	12 29 x 11 x x
8. Another word for rock	_ _ _ _ _	13 x x 14 x
9. Betraying your country	_ _ _ _ _ _ _ _	12 27 x x 13 x 23
10. A school subject	_ _ _ _	15 x x 16
11. An animal you ride	_ _ _ _ _	18 x 17 x x
12. The red planet	_ _ _ _	5 x 27 x
13. The planet we live on	_ _ _ _ _	x 26 x x 1
14. One twelfth of the year	_ _ _ _ _	19 x 14 x x
15. Another word for wander	_ _ _ _ _	20 x 28 19
16. The land near water	_ _ _ _ _	21 x 7 x x
17. Fly like an eagle	_ _ _ _	22 x x 9
18. A bad skin condition	_ _ _ _	2 x 21 x
19. Sound like an owl	_ _ _ _	1 10 11 x
20. The opposite of lengthen	_ _ _ _ _ _ _	22 x x x x 4 23
21. Why you did something	_ _ _ _ _ _	17 x x 22 x 14
22. A snake's poison	_ _ _ _ _	24 x 23 x 15
23. A fuzzy pet	_ _ _ _ _ _ _	29 x 25 x 6 x x
24. Choose your government	_ _ _ _ _	24 8 x x
25. Inclement weather	_ _ _ _ _	13 x 3 20 x
26. A nation's song	_ _ _ _ _ _	28 x x 16 x 25
27. A safe place	_ _ _ _ _	18 24 x 23

People: Appearance and personality

People and appearance

VOCABULARY

acne/pimples	good-looking	pretty
average build	handsome	rosy cheeks
average height	in (good) shape	scar
bald	long eyelashes	shaved head
bangs	long/short hair	short
beard	mole	skinny
blond/brown hair	muscular	slender
blue/brown eyes	mustache	slim
braces	out of shape	stocky
bushy eyebrows	overweight	tall
curly/straight hair	pale complexion	tan
dark complexion	(physically) fit	tattoo
dry/oily skin	pierced ears	wart
freckles	pigtails	well-built
glasses	ponytail	wrinkles

PUZZLE 5·1

Collocation match up: Appearance *The following words and phrases can be used to describe someone's appearance. Some of the expressions require is and some require has: He is bald and She **has** bangs. Decide which of the two verbs, is or has, belong with each expression and write it in the blank.*

1. _____ acne/pimples

2. _____ bald

3. _____ blond/brown hair

4. _____ bushy eyebrows

5. _____ dry/oily skin

6. _____ good-looking

7. _____ long eyelashes

8. _____ muscular

9. _____ overweight

10. _____ pierced ears

11. _____ pretty

12. _____ a shaved head	29. _____ a tan
13. _____ slender	30. _____ well-built
14. _____ tall	31. _____ average heightz
15. _____ a wart	32. _____ a beard
16. _____ average build	33. _____ braces
17. _____ bangs	34. _____ a dark complexion
18. _____ blue/brown eyes	35. _____ glasses
19. _____ curly/straight hair	36. _____ in (good) shape
20. _____ freckles	37. _____ a mole
21. _____ handsome	38. _____ out of shape
22. _____ long/short hair	39. _____ (physically) fit
23. _____ a mustache	40. _____ a ponytail
24. _____ a pale complexion	41. _____ a scar
25. _____ pigtails	42. _____ skinny
26. _____ rosy cheeks	43. _____ stocky
27. _____ short	44. _____ a tattoo
28. _____ slim	45. _____ wrinkles

PUZZLE 5·2

Definition match up: Appearance *Match the following definitions with the words in the vocabulary box.*

1. A black circle on your skin _____

2. Things that straighten teeth _____

3. Lines that come with age _____

4. A mark left on skin after a cut _____

5. Artwork on someone's skin _____

6. Short with broad shoulders _____

7. Hair that covers your forehead _____

8. Brown spots on your face _____

9. No hair because of hair loss _____

10. No hair because of a haircut _____

11. Not short and not tall _____

12. Not slim and not overweight _____

Labeling: Physical appearance *Attach the physical appearance–related labels to these lists of words.*

build	fitness level	hairstyle
complexion	general appearance	height
facial hair	hair length	skin blemish

1. _____

in (good) shape
out of shape
(physically) fit

2. _____

goatee
mustache
sideburns

3. _____

mole
pimple
wart

4. _____

short
average height
tall

5. _____

slender
stocky
overweight

6. _____

long
short
shoulder-length

7. _____

oily skin
dry skin
rosy cheeks

8. _____

bangs
shoulder-length hair
ponytail

9. _____

attractive
handsome
pretty

Fill in the blanks: Appearance *Complete the following paragraphs by filling in the blanks using the words provided.*

Describing hairstyles

bald	curly	older
blond	dye	shave
braids	hair	shoulder-length

When describing a person's _____, you can talk about color, length, and style.

Hair comes in many colors such as brown, _____, red, and black. Of course, if

you want to change your hair color, you can always _____ it another color.

Sometimes, as people grow _____, their hair turns gray or white. And some people lose their hair altogether and go _____. Along with color, you can also describe someone's hair by its length. There is short hair, long hair, and _____ hair. Some people even _____ their heads. When describing someone's hair, you can also mention whether it's straight, wavy, or _____ and other features such as bangs, _____, pigtails, or ponytails.

Complexion

blemishes	light	ruddy
clear	oily	scar
complexion	rosy	skin

The color, texture, and quality of a person's skin is called _____. Some people have a dark complexion, while others have a _____ or even a pale complexion. If you have healthy looking red cheeks, people say you have a _____ or _____ complexion. Complexion is more than just _____ color, however. Some people have dry skin whereas others have _____ skin. Some people have _____ such as pimples or warts while others have _____ skin with no blemishes. And sometimes after an injury such as a cut or a burn, a _____ will remain on the skin.

Fitness level

activity	exercise	fitness	shape	watch
balanced	fit	out	spend	work

When describing people we can also talk about their _____ level. People who _____ out a lot and _____ what they eat tend to be in good _____. Regular _____ and a _____ diet are an important part of staying physically _____. On the other hand, people who _____ hours in front of computers or TVs, rarely doing any physical _____, tend to be _____ of shape.

Language and appearance

acceptable	imply	issue	stereotypes
build	insensitive	neutral	

The language you use to describe a person can be a very sensitive _____. For example, saying that a woman "has blond hair" is _____, but saying that a woman "is a blonde" may not be. This is because there is a history of offensive _____ depicting women with blond hair as being unintelligent. Therefore, calling a woman "a blonde" can also _____ that she is not very smart. Saying she "has blond hair," on the other hand, is just a simple comment on her hair color. Similar issues arise when discussing a person's body shape, or _____.

Calling someone fat or short can come across as very _____ and even rude. The term overweight can be considered a _____ term, but some people don't like that and may prefer terms like heavy, heavyset, or large.

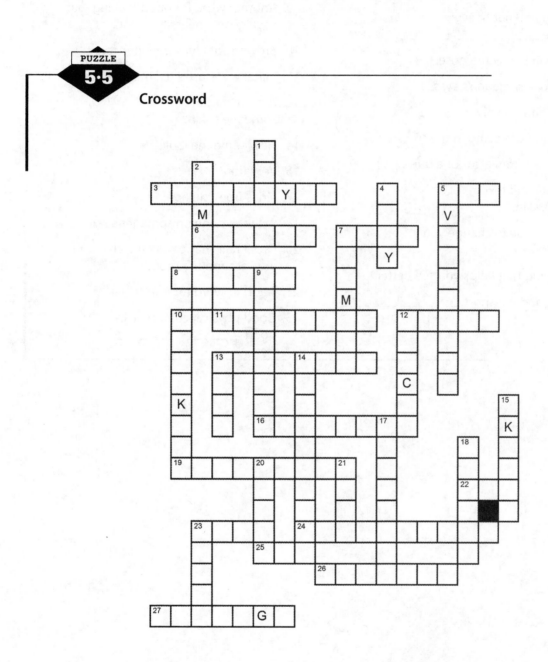

PUZZLE
5·5

Crossword

Across

3. What someone's hair looks like.

5. Poor physical condition: _____ of shape.

6. Another word for good-looking, but usually only refers to a woman.

Down

1. Good physical condition: Physically _____.

2. Small red spots on someone's skin caused by acne.

4. The opposite of dry skin: _____ skin.

Across (cont.)

7. Having no hair due to hair loss.

8. How tall you are.

11. Hair that is tied at the back.

12. Not thin and not heavy: Average _____.

13. Facial hair below the nose.

16. Hair above someone's eyes.

19. Hair on the side of someone's face.

22. Dark skin from being in the sun.

23. A mark left from a cut or a burn.

24. The color and texture of a person's skin.

25. What you use to change your hair color.

26. Something that helps you see better.

27. Not tall and not short: _____ height.

Down (cont.)

5. The opposite of slim.

7. A problem on someone's skin like a wart or a pimple.

9. Another word for good-looking, but usually only refers to a man.

10. Brown spots on someone's face.

12. Metal wires used to straighten teeth.

13. A black, raised circle on someone's skin.

14. How someone looks.

15. Very thin.

17. Lines from old age.

18. Artwork done on someone's skin.

20. Facial hair that covers the chin and area around the mouth.

21. Another word for thin.

23. Good physical condition: In good _____.

5·6

Word search: Appearance *Find the following words in the grid.*

```
O V E R W E I G H T O I L Y S K I N Y N A N S S
P X R Q I D L G E N T H S K R H P T I R E L Y B
P I E R C E D E A R S F C Q L N T N W D I V V O
R D M O U S G T A T T O O L T E Y I L A T B R E
G U U P R V H W S L I M A N R A S D T S A S E S
L S S L L Z L O B B H T H P H S N Y E Y K L O N
A T T X Y E R M R H B N R B E M N N R E W Y S E
S O A B S A S R I T T Y B V E O S L E N D E R L
S C C T C E Y E B R O W S Z P E I H O D D Z T W
E K H S S B W Q H A N D S O M E C J H G R R R P
S Y E K P L R W X T L S M H W Y X L U N E F I Q
M U M I I I I D K E G D M U S C U L A R R S L K
O B B N D V N B B N R I C O M P L E X I O N Y B
L R E N C O K S A A V E R A G E B U I L D M M Y
E A A Y L D L B H H L I A E O U T O F S H A P E
V C R B K Z E O R A A N L S H A V E D H E A D L
S E D X E F S Q S H P A V E R A G E H E I G H T
P S T R A I G H T C P E F R E C K L E S X T P G
```

Average build	In shape	Shaved head
Average height	Mole	Short
Bald	Muscular	Skinny
Bangs	Mustache	Slender
Beard	Oily skin	Slim
Blond	Out of shape	Stocky
Braces	Overweight	Straight
Complexion	Pale	Tall
Curly	Pierced ears	Tanned
Eyebrows	Pimples	Tattoo
Freckles	Ponytail	Wart
Glasses	Pretty	Wrinkles
Hair	Rosy cheeks	
Handsome	Scar	

People: Appearance and personality **51**

People and personality

Personality traits

affectionate	bossy	considerate	frugal	obnoxious	reckless
ambitious	brave	courageous	hardworking	optimistic	reliable
arrogant	brilliant	creative	heartless	outgoing	selfish
articulate	clever	deceitful	messy	patient	stingy
artistic	confident	easygoing	moody	picky	stubborn
athletic	conservative	emotional	narrow-minded	punctual	whiney
					witty

PUZZLE 5·7

Definition matching: Personality traits *Choose a trait from the vocabulary list that could complete the definition sentences below.*

1. _____ people often tell you what to do.

2. _____ people play a lot of sports.

3. _____ people feel they have the ability to do something.

4. _____ people hate to waste anything.

5. _____ people are usually on time.

6. _____ people think only of themselves.

7. _____ people rarely change their minds.

8. _____ people complain about everything.

9. _____ people don't mind waiting.

PUZZLE 5·8

Synonym matching: Personality traits *Choose a word from the personality vocabulary list that is a synonym for the following words.*

1. sociable _____

2. intelligent _____

3. rude _____

4. conceited _____

5. well-spoken _____

6. thoughtful _____

7. dependable _____

8. cruel _____

Antonym matching: Personality traits *Choose a word from the personality trait list that could be an antonym for the following words.*

1. honest _____

2. lazy _____

3. open-minded _____

4. uptight _____

5. neat _____

6. shy _____

7. rational _____

8. pessimistic _____

Antonym prefixes: Personality traits *Use one of the following prefixes to make the antonyms of the words in the box:* dis-, im-, in-, *and* un-.

1. _____ patient

2. _____ honest

3. _____ reliable

4. _____ sociable

5. _____ considerate

6. _____ loyal

Word paths: Personality traits *Find and circle the secret words by following a connected path through the maze. Some words may overlap. Then use the remaining letters to uncover an idiom related to people.*

C	A	S	T	I	M	O	O	D	Y	R
O	■	M	■	N	■	O	■	V	■	E
N	S	I	E	G	Y	I	R	A	I	L
A	■	D	■	N	■	M	■	B	■	D
T	R	E	I	T	A	P	O	L	E	H
T	■	N	■	S	■	H	■	I	■	O
E	M	T	P	U	N	C	E	T	A	N
S	■	S	■	S	■	T	■	K	■	E
S	Y	E	Y	H	R	U	A	L	T	S
H	■	L	■	E	■	D	■	R	■	L
S	I	F	D	E	C	E	I	T	F	U

1. Can be depended on. __ __ __ __ __ __ __ __ __

2. Hates to spend money. __ __ __ __ __ __ __

3. Thinks of other people. __ __ __ __ __ __ __ __ __ __ __ __

4. Often gloomy, depressed, or angry. __ __ __ __ __ __

5. Can't stand waiting for anything. __ __ __ __ __ __ __ __ __ __

6. Says, "Please," and "Thank you." __ __ __ __ __ __ __

7. Leaves clothes and books everywhere. __ __ __ __ __

8. Misleads people and tells lies. __ __ __ __ __ __ __ __ __

9. Never late for anything. __ __ __ __ __ __ __ __

10. Never tells lies. __ __ __ __ __ __

11. Thinks only of himself or herself. __ __ __ __ __ __ __

12. Feels uncomfortable around people. __ __ __

13. Impolite. __ __ __ __ __

Hidden message: Personality idiom: *What do you call a very influential person who can make things happen?*

__   __ __ __ __ __   __ __ __   __ __ __ __ __ __

Word search: Personality traits *Find the following words in the grid.*

```
O B N O X I O U S N A R R O W M I N D E D B D U
B D A A F M C D E P E N D A B L E C X Q J I G J
R X M I H L S E L F I S H R A G C R E A T I V E
I K B A F F E C T I O N A T E M O T I O N A L E
L E I E F Y M E H D E C E I T F U L G O F L B A
L X T B Y N U P A F C O N S E R V A T I V E B D
I O I H O N E S T S K E A T H L E T I C O C Q E
A U O I N X B O S S Y H W I N T E L L I G E N T
N T U R E L I A B L E G A C G E N E R O U S T L
T G S X R D Y T A H Y T O R I M O O D Y P Z U L
W O E P V E N G Y C O N F I D E N T Y S E F S C
U I F R N E U S T U B B O R N W P U N C T U A L
P N T I I R M E M E S S Y L B G O E R H A Y C A
I G H T F Z H E A R T L E S S C Q R G Q N U N H
C W A A Y I A R T I C U L A T E O U K Z T Y Q Q
K P A R R O G A N T R B U V D Q O C I I R L H S
Y J F B S G P S O C I A B L E H R U D E N Y Q D
C O N S I D E R A T E O A K T H L S T I N G Y B
```

Affectionate	Dependable	Patient
Ambitious	Easygoing	Picky
Arrogant	Emotional	Punctual
Articulate	Frugal	Reliable
Artistic	Generous	Rude
Athletic	Hardworking	Selfish
Bossy	Heartless	Sociable
Brilliant	Honest	Stingy
Confident	Intelligent	Stubborn
Conservative	Messy	Thoughtful
Considerate	Moody	Whiney
Creative	Narrow-minded	Witty
Cruel	Obnoxious	
Deceitful	Outgoing	

Crossword

Across

2. _____ people think they are better than other people.

5. A _____ person is someone who is always on time.

10. Another word for brave.

12. A _____ person is someone who thinks bad things will happen in the future.

14. An _____ person is someone who doesn't lie.

15. A _____ person is someone who makes people laugh.

Down

1. The opposite of lazy.

3. A _____ person is someone you can depend on.

4. An _____ person plays sports and does lots of exercise.

6. Another word for considerate.

7. A _____ person is someone who sees the good in everything.

8. Another word for clever.

9. An _____ person is someone who likes to meet people.

Across (cont.)

16. A _____ person is someone who wants to have everything.

19. A _____ person is someone who doesn't work very hard.

24. A _____ person is someone who doesn't keep his or her house clean.

26. A _____ person is someone who says, "Please," and "Thank you."

27. A _____ person misleads others or lies to them.

28. A _____ person is someone who doesn't like to spend any money.

31. A _____ person is someone who thinks of other people and does things for them.

32. A _____ person is someone who is giving and sharing.

Down (cont.)

11. Another word for smart.

13. A _____ person is someone who feels uncomfortable meeting new people.

17. The opposite of polite.

18. An _____ person is someone who is easy to get along with.

20. A _____ person is someone who is not afraid to do something.

21. A _____ person is someone who is nice to other people.

22. An _____ person hates waiting for anything.

23. A _____ person is someone who thinks up original ideas.

25. A _____ person is someone who thinks only of himself or herself.

29. A _____ person is someone who keeps his or her house clean.

30. A _____ person is someone who has lots of experience and knowledge.

Idiom puzzle: Personality idioms *Complete the following personality-related idioms. Use the shape symbols below the blanks to help you solve the missing blanks.*

1. A person who watches TV all day: A _ _ _ _ _ _ P O T A T O
   9 ■ ♦ ▲

2. Someone who enjoys the mornings: A N   E A R L Y _ _ _ _ _
   ● ♠ 7 ♥

3. A person who stays up late: A _ _ _ _ _ O W L
   11 ♠   16 Σ

4. An enthusiastic person: A N   E A G E R _ _ _ _ _
   ● ★ 17   ★ ◐

5. A person who causes problems: A _ _ _ _ _ _ _ _ _ _ _
   22 ◑ 13 ♦ ● ♣ ★ Ω ⊡ △ ★ ◐

6. Someone who interferes in another's business: A _ _ _ _ _ _ _
   ● ♦ 23   ● ■ ♥

7. An ambitious hardworking person: A _ _ _ - _ _ _ _ _ _
   19 ■   ★ Σ 14 ★ ◐

8. A really clever person: A _ _ _ _ C O O K I E
   28 Ω 6 ◑ Σ

9. A young genius: A   W H I Z _ _ _
   △ ♠ 8

10. A dangerously unpredictable person: A   L O O S E _ _ _ _ _
    ▲ ⊡ 12 18 ■ ▼

11. Someone with their head in the clouds: A _ _ _ _ _ _ _ _ _ _
    ♥ ⊡   ♥ ⊡ 20 ⊡ Ω ★ ◐

12. A bad person: A   R O T T E N _ _ _
    1   5 ♣ ★

13. Someone who likes to talk: A _ _ _ _ _ _ _ _
    ▲   10 Σ 27 ★ ◑ ● ■

14. A person who is very pleased: A   H A P P Y _ _ _ _ _
    15 ⊡ Ω 25 ★ ◐

15. Someone who annoys you: A   P A I N   I N   T H E _ _ _
    ▼ 3 ▲

16. A relatively unimportant person: A _ _ _ _ _ F R Y
    24 Ω ⊡ ♣ ♣

17. A bad person who seems good: A _ _ _ _   I N   S H E E P' S   C L O T H I N G
    26 ♣

18. Someone who is a little strange: A N _ _ _ _ _ _ _
    ■ ♥ ♥ ● ⊡ 2 ♣

19. A very outgoing person: A _ _ _ _ _ _   B U T T E R F L Y
    4 ▲ 21 ⊡ ♣

Code breaker: A personality proverb *Use the number codes in puzzle 5·14 to solve this proverb.*

People cannot change their character:

_ _ _ _ _ _ _ _   _ _ _ _ _ _   _ _ _ _ _ _   _ _ _   _ _ _ _ _
1   2 3 4 5 6 7 8   9 10 11 12 13 14   15 16 17 18 19 20   21 22 23   24 25 26 27 28

Travel

VOCABULARY

airline	customs	luggage	sightseeing
amenities	departure	monument	souvenir
arrival	destination	nightlife	temple
attraction	duty-free	one-way	tour
backpacking	exotic	overhead bin	tourist
board/embark	festival	passport	travel agent
budget	flight	postcard	trekking
carry-on	handicrafts	reservation	vacancy
castle	journey	resort	visa
cuisine	landmark	round-trip	voyage
currency	local		

PUZZLE 6·1

Definition match up: Travel *The words in the vocabulary list are all related to travel. Look up any words you don't know. Find one word that could fit each definition.*

1. Bags, backpacks, and suitcases _____

2. Luggage you bring with you onto the plane _____

3. A document that shows your nationality _____

4. A document you need to enter a country _____

5. A sign that means rooms are available _____

6. Another way to say food _____

7. Inexpensive (and often low quality) _____

8. A picture you can write a short letter on _____

9. The place where you are going _____

10. A ticket that goes to and from a destination _____

11. A journey by sea _____

12. Get on a ship or plane _____

13. Something you buy to remember your trip _____

14. Things to do or see in the evening _____

15. A statue or building that commemorates something famous _____

16. An easily recognizable structure such as a monument or building _____

17. A person who is traveling for pleasure _____

18. Money used in a country _____

19. Action of leaving _____

20. A journey by airplane _____

Labeling: Travel *Attach the travel-related labels to these lists of words.*

accommodations	landmarks	ticket types
baggage	people who work for airlines	tourism-related businesses
gift shop purchases	people who work in an airport	tourist activities

1. _____

airport security
baggage handlers
customs officers

2. _____

backpack
carry-on
luggage

3. _____

pilots
flight attendants
ticketing agents

4. _____

business
economy
first class

5. _____

magazines for the flight
postcards
souvenirs

6. _____

bridges
castles
temples

7. _____

bed and breakfast
hotel
youth hostel

8. _____

airlines
hotels
tour operators

9. _____

trekking
sightseeing
shopping for gifts

Fill in the blanks: Travel *Complete the following paragraphs by, filling in the blanks using the words provided.*

Catching a flight

arrive	boarding	duty	lounge	security
bags	check-in	flight	passed	show

When catching an international _____, it's important to _____ at the airport early because there are often delays and lineups. First, you head to the _____ counter where an airline representative checks your ID and tickets. If everything is satisfactory, you check your _____ at the counter and the representative gives you your _____ pass. Next, you have to pass through airport _____ to make sure you aren't carrying anything dangerous. You will be required to _____ your ID again as well as your boarding pass. Once you have _____ security, you usually wait for your flight in a _____ near the boarding gate. If you have extra time, you can go shopping at the _____-free shops.

Traveling on a budget

airline	budget	locals	package	tourists
backpack	guesthouses	markets	public	track

Hotels and _____ tickets can be prohibitively expensive, so many travelers try to find ways to travel on a _____. Many travelers opt to _____ around a country instead of staying in a resort area and paying for expensive _____ tours. These backpackers often stay at small _____ and use _____ transportation to get around. As well, they try to avoid restaurants that cater to _____ because prices are usually inflated at those restaurants. Instead, they eat where the _____ eat and shop in the local _____. As well, they avoid tourist traps and head somewhere off the beaten _____.

Traveling in style

amenities	entertainment	money	stress	swimming
cruise	inclusive	star	style	

If _____ is no object and you can afford to travel in _____, then you can avoid a lot of the hassle of backpacking. There are many five-_____ hotels that will go out of their way to make your stay a relaxing, _____-free vacation. There are also all-_____ resorts, where you pay one price up front to enjoy

all of the _____ of the resort. Another option for luxury travel is to take a
_____ on a cruise ship. Cruise ships have everything from _____
pools to daily onboard _____.

Experiencing the local culture

| cuisine | experience | history | markets | wares |
| exotic | festivals | live | spices | |

One of the great benefits of travel is that you can _____ another culture.
Traveling offers you the opportunity to sample the flavors of the local _____.
You can try _____ dishes made with _____ and ingredients
you wouldn't normally eat. You can also head to the local _____ to shop for
indigenous _____ such as jewelry or clothing. You can visit the museums and
galleries to learn more about the _____ and art of the region. And you can
participate in _____ that celebrate the traditional culture of the region. It also
offers you a chance to see how other people _____.

Crossword

Across

1. A sandy place next to the ocean.

8. Something you buy to remember your trip.

9. A time when people don't have to work.

10. Food delivered right to your room: Room _____.

12. An easily recognizable structure such as a monument or a building.

13. Get into a country: _____ through customs.

14. Another word for trip.

Down

2. The food indigenous to a region: the local _____.

3. Walk up a mountain.

4. A bag that you carry on your back.

5. A holiday or vacation on a ship.

6. A ticket that is good for both ways: _____ trip.

7. The time when your flight lands: _____ time.

9. A trip for newlyweds.

11. A popular place for vacations.

Across (cont.)

16. A place where you board ships.

17. A form of transportation that goes on tracks.

18. A place where you board a bus or a train.

19. A time when kids don't go to school.

22. _____ your tickets in advance.

24. The time when your flight leaves: _____ time.

26. A place to buy souvenirs: _____ shop.

29. The place where you are heading.

31. A piece of identification that you need to travel abroad.

32. A document you need to enter a country.

33. A place where people sleep while on vacation.

34. _____ your bags before you get onto a plane.

35. Bags, backpacks, and suitcases.

Down (cont.)

15. A place where you board a flight.

16. A place to swim in your hotel.

20. A person who is travelling.

21. The kind of ticket you buy when you are not coming back. (3-3)

23. A person who books tickets for you: A travel _____.

25. A hard, rectangular piece of luggage with a handle.

27. An airplane journey from one place to another.

28. A hotel that you drive to.

30. _____ some identification at the ticket counter.

31. Get ready to go: _____ your bags.

Word search: Travel *Find the following words in the grid.*

```
E R O U N D T R I P A K Q F L I G H T J O C E O
R M H R C V O V O Y A G E A T T R A C T I O N V
J J B P A T V N X K U K C B A C K P A C K I N G
D E P A R T U R E X J O U R N E Y O A H E N E O
P A G Y R X U N L W L D C W V L R Z M L W G Z L
O D P D I K G V A C A N C Y B R P Q P S A Z A Z
S Q D J V O B C A R R Y O N B Z W M E G O V V J
T D E C A N P W N I G H T L I F E I G K I K S O
C Y S A L T R A V E L A G E N T T U R T T M R G
A K T S I Z Z R S F G D Z T A I L A S C O T N D
R C I T D R U A A S R A M O N U M E N T R I Z D
D U N L U O L S H A P E R E S D F T S O K J G S
N I A E T H I I O B E O M R N T H U S K I P P U
K S T H Y V O B N Z U A R A E I C E E E V N M A
P I I Q F C F H U E F D L T C U R R E N C Y D X
X N O B R A J P W V J D G C V S T E P P T X R I
B E N D E B X S I G H T S E E I N G L G M W S P
V E O V E R H E A D B I N F T S O U V E N I R R
```

Airline · Amenities · Arrival · Attraction · Backpacking · Board · Budget · Carry-on · Castle · Cuisine · Currency · Customs · Departure · Destination · Duty-free · Embark · Festival · Flight · Journey · Landmark · Local · Luggage · Monument · Nightlife · One-way · Overhead bin · Passport · Postcard · Resort · Round-trip · Sightseeing · Souvenir · Temple · Tour · Travel agent · Trekking · Vacancy · Visa · Voyage

Idiom puzzle: Travel expressions *Complete the following travel-related expressions. Use the shape symbols below the blanks to help you solve the missing spaces.*

1. Pay for your flight in advance:

_ _ _ _ _ YOUR TICKETS
△ ♦ 24 ♥

2. Hand your luggage to the airlines:

_ _ _ _ _ _ YOUR BAGS
♣ 17 ▲ 23 ♥

3. Call ahead to get a place to sleep:

_ _ _ _ _ A RESERVATION
25 ◑ ♥ ▲

4. Have food brought to you:

_ _ _ _ _ ROOM SERVICE
21 ♠ Ω ▲ 11

5. Wait at the check-in counter:

_ _ _ _ _ IN LINE
5 ⊡ ◑ Σ 13

6. Enter a country:

_ _ _ _ _ CUSTOMS
♣ ★ ▲ 8 ♠

7. Go shopping inside the airport:

_ _ _ _ _ _ _ _ DUTY-FREE
▼ ■ ♠ ♣ 7 ◑ ● 26

8. Ask for permission to go to a country:

_ _ _ _ _ FOR A VISA
◑ ▼ ▼ ◑ 20

9. Wave your arm at a taxi:

_ _ _ _ A CAB
▽ ◑ 12 ★

10. Get ready to go on vacation:

_ _ _ _ _ YOUR BAGS
▼ ◑ 1 ♥

11. Get some transportation:

_ _ _ _ A CAR
♠ ▲ Σ 9

12. A sign that lights up during turbulence:

_ _ _ _ _ _ _ YOUR SEATBELT
◑ ● 27 ▲ 19

13. See the sights:

_ _ _ _ _ A TOUR
30 ◑ ♥ 15

14. A sign on a hotel doorknob:

DO NOT _ _ _ _ _ _ _
Ω 29 ● ⊡ 22 2 △

15. Get some foreign currency:

_ _ _ _ _ _ _ _ SOME MONEY
▲   ♣ ▽ ◑ Σ 14 18

16. Put your carry-on in a safe place:

_ _ _ _ _ YOUR LUGGAGE
● ⊡ 3

17. Prove who you are:

_ _ _ _ _ SOME IDENTIFICATION
4 ▽ ♦ 16

18. Get on the aircraft:

_ _ _ _ _ _ THE PLANE
10 28 ◑ ♠ Ω

19. Make sure you don't sleep too late:

_ _ _ _ _ _ _ A WAKE-UP CALL
♠ ▲   ■ ▲ ● 6

Code breaker: A proverb about travel *Use the number code in puzzle 6·6 to solve the proverb.*

Deal with a problem if it arises and do not worry about it until it does.

— — — — —   — — — —   — — — — — —   — — — —   — — —
1 2 3 4 5   6 7 8 9   10 11 12 13 14 15   16 17 18 19   20 21 22

— — — —   — —   — —
23 24 25 26 27 28 29 30

Sports

VOCABULARY

amateur	draw	pass	sportsmanship
athlete	equipment	record	stadium
champion	foul	referee	tackle
coach	judge	rules	tournament
compete	league	score	training
competitor	match	serve	trophy
court	offense	spectator	
defense	opponent		

PUZZLE 7·1

Word list: Sports *The words in the vocabulary box are related to sports. Look up any of the words you don't know and then find a word that could match each definition to the right.*

1. A person who participates in sports _____

2. An athlete who does not get paid _____

3. Practice and preparation for sports _____

4. Things used to play sports _____

5. The best score or time _____

6. A group of teams that play against each other _____

7. A person who watches sports _____

8. A competition where many teams play against each other to determine a winner _____

9. The winner of a tournament _____

10. One game between opponents _____

11. An action that is against the rules in sports _____

12. Fair play and a good attitude _____

13. What the champions take home _____

14. A place where sports like soccer are played _____

15. A place where sports like basketball are played _____

16. A person who oversees the training of an athlete or a sports team _____

17. A person who determines a winner in gymnastics or diving _____

18. Attempts to score a point _____

19. The opposite of offense _____

20. How many points each team has _____

Labeling: Sports *Attach the sports-related labels to the following lists of words.*

athletes
examples of fouls
people who help athletes

places where sports are played
sporting events
sports equipment

sports you "do"
sports you "play"
variations of "throw"

1. _____

gymnastics
karate

2. _____

offside
tripping

3. _____

court
field

4. _____

boxer
gymnast

5. _____

coach
trainer

6. _____

gloves
mouth guard

7. _____

lob
toss

8. _____

match
tournament

9. _____

basketball
rugby

Fill in the blanks: Sports *Complete the following paragraphs by filling in the blanks using the words provided.*

Training

balanced	endurance	injury	professional
competitiveness	hone	lift	work

_____ athletes require extensive training to achieve a high level of _____. They _____ out and _____ weights to gain strength and _____. They practice constantly to _____ their skills. They eat a _____ diet to get the nutrition and energy needed to compete. Finally, before a competition, they warm up to prevent _____.

Sportsmanship

arguing	breaks	fair	injuring	rules
attitude	decision	faking	intentionally	

Sportsmanship is a sense of _____ play and maintaining a good _____ toward winning and losing. Good sportsmanship involves following the _____ of the game. Though everybody accidentally _____ rules from time to time, breaking the rules _____ is considered poor sportsmanship. Good sportsmanship also involves accepting the referee's _____ even when you do not agree with it. _____ with the referee, on the other hand, is considered poor sportsmanship. The worst examples of poor sportsmanship are intentionally _____ another player or _____ an injury yourself in order to get another player penalized.

Tournaments

awarded	champion	elimination	tournament
ceremonies	compete	sole	trophy

A _____ is a competition in which athletes or teams of athletes compete against each other to determine a _____. In many tournaments, there are _____ rounds in which losing teams are knocked out of the tournament and winning teams go on to _____ against other winning teams until finally there is a _____ survivor. In many tournaments there is a _____ that is _____ to the champion during the closing _____.

Doping

advertising	blood	doping	pressure
ban	disqualified	enhance	titles

Professional athletes are under a lot of _____ to do well in competitions. Success in major sporting events can mean millions of dollars in _____ contracts from sponsors. And so, some athletes take drugs that _____ their performance. This practice is known as _____. Most international sports organizations _____ the use of performance-enhancing drugs. These organizations require athletes to give _____ and urine samples after the competitions. Athletes who are caught doping are _____ from sporting events and often have their _____ stripped from them.

Crossword

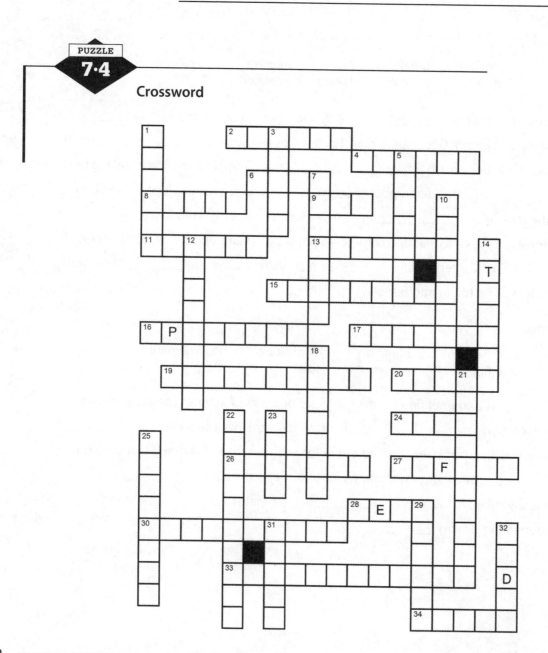

Across

2. A team sport played on ice.

4. Something the champions get to take home.

6. If you _____ the ball, you throw it to your teammate.

8. A place where tennis matches and basketball games are played.

9. A score in which each team has the same number of points.

11. The best score or time ever.

13. Attempts to prevent opponents from scoring.

15. Things that athletes need to play a sport.

16. The person or team you play against.

17. Something the referee blows.

19. A special event in which many teams play each other.

20. To begin a match in volleyball or tennis, someone has to _____ the ball.

24. An action that is against the rules in sports.

26. An athlete who does not get paid to play.

27. Another word for beat.

28. If you _____ your opponent, then you win.

30. A sport in which athletes throw a ball through a hoop.

33. An athlete who gets paid to play.

34. The number of points that each team has.

Down

1. A team sport in which athletes kick a ball.

3. A person who tells a team what to do.

5. Attempts to score points.

7. A place where soccer and baseball games are held.

10. A person who watches a sporting event.

12. A winner in a tournament.

14. A person who plays sports.

18. A person who makes sure both teams play fairly.

21. A team sport in which athletes hit a ball over a net using their hands.

22. A person who protects the net.

23. Another way to say, "A tie."

25. A sport in which people hit a ball with a bat.

29. A sport in which athletes hit a ball over a net using a racket.

31. Goalkeepers try to _____ shots.

32. A person who chooses the winner in sports like gymnastics.

Word search: Sports *Find the words below in the grid.*

```
T G T O U R N A M E N T P D C S S C Q R D L D E
B Y P S L Q P U J N B M S P C D P H E S I E B A
Q M M S Z N O H U B Y S A E T U O A L Z V Q B L
B N B C A L L Y D C A O H T A J R M V L F V M M
V A C O E H Z T G P E C O A C H T P V A O L F F
P S N R S E R V E U G C C Q K H S I F L I H H D
B T F E X W N B G N T E K Z L A M O S W C A V W
A I G A E H O A A D N R E L E T A N F H A D P Z
S C O M N O E L L H M I Y X G H N D E F E N S E
K S P A R L F V R U V E S N U L S D M G Z W G W
E C P T C E P F I F C W I L Y E H D F V Q P S G
T E O E C N C D E N R N D H R T I D A X E P E I
B R N U C O A O I N I F P Z U E P N I E C F E N
A U E R O T M J R A S O F J F R C F R K G K S J
L L N S M A P R D R E D C O M P E T I T O R N
L E T C O U R T E T R B T T U N F U M J M F K Z
Y S N G D C C C O T E A I O L E Q U I P M E N T
G O A L K E E P E R E D W P R B A S E B A L L W
```

Amateur	Defense	Match	Soccer
Athlete	Draw	Offense	Spectator
Baseball	Equipment	Opponent	Sportsmanship
Basketball	Foul	Pass	Stadium
Champion	Goalkeeper	Record	Tackle
Coach	Gymnastics	Referee	Tennis
Compete	Hockey	Rules	Tournament
Competitor	Judge	Score	Training
Court	League	Serve	Trophy

Idiom puzzle: Sports idioms and expressions *Complete the following sports-related idioms. Use the shape symbols below the blanks to help you solve the missing spaces.*

Then use the number code to solve the following proverb.

1. Make a mistake: D R O P   T H E __ __ __ __ __
    ♦ 22 ★ ★

2. A fair competition: A   L E V E L   P L A Y I N G __ __ __ __ __ __
    Ω ○ ♥ ★ 7

3. A rough estimate: __ __ __ __ __ __ __ __   F I G U R E
    ♦ ♣ ★ 2 ● ♣ 21 ♦

4. Do something that surprises someone: T H R O W   A __ __ __ __ __ __   B A L L
    ■ ♠ ◐ 20

5. As expected: P A R   F O R   T H E __ __ __ __ __ __ __
    ■ ▼ ♠ ◑ 1 ♥

6. Give up: __ __ __ __ __   I N   T H E   T O W E L
    ⊡ 19 ◐ ▼ 4

7. In a situation you can't handle: O U T   O F   Y O U R __ __ __ __ __ __
    ★ ♥ 11 ▲ ♠ ♥

8. The deadline is approaching: I T ' S   A __ __ __ __ __   A G A I N S T   T I M E
    ◑ ♣ ■ 10

9. Do something risky: __ __ __ __ __ __   O N   T H I N   I C E
    Σ ◈ 5 18 ♥

10. Getting perfect results: __ __ __ __ __ __ __   A   T H O U S A N D
    ♦ ♣ ⊡ 9 ○ 16 ▲

11. Struggling and not doing well: O N   T H E __ __ __ __ __ __
    ◑ ▼ ● ♥ 8

12. Lost a struggle: D O W N   F O R   T H E __ __ __ __ __
    ■ ▼ ♠ 6 ⊡

13. A completely different situation: A __ __ __ __ __   N E W   B A L L   G A M E
    14 △ ▼ ★ ♥

14. Prepare for every possibility: C O V E R   A L L   Y O U R __ __ __ __ __
    ♦ ♣ Σ ♥ 17

15. It's your turn to make a decision: T H E   B A L L   I S   I N   Y O U R __ __ __ __ __
    23 ▼ ♠ ◑ ⊡

16. Be exactly right: H I T   T H E __ __ __ __ __ ' __ - __ __ __
    ♦ ♠ ★ ★ Σ ♥ 13 ♥

17. Without any kind of restraint: N O __ __ __ __ __ __   B A R R E D
    △ ▼ ★ 12 Σ

18. Think a crime may have been committed: S U S P E C T __ __ __ __ __   P L A Y
    Ω 3 ♠ ★

19. A powerful or influential person: A   H E A V Y __ __ __ __ __ __
    △ 15 ⊡ ⊡ 24 ◐

Code breaker: A proverb about competition: *Advice for rabbits (and tortoises):*

__ __ __ __   __ __ __   __ __ __ __ __ __   __ __ __ __   __ __ __   __ __ __ __
1 2 3 4   5 6 7   8 9 10 11 12 13   14 15 16 17   18 19 20   21 22 23 24

Word paths: Sports *Find and circle the secret words by following a connected path through the maze. Some words may overlap.*

A	M	A	L	E	A	G	N	M	U	I
O	■	T	■	B	■	U	■	O	■	D
R	U	E	F	E	T	E	L	H	T	A
D	■	D	■	N	■	Y	■	L	■	T
O	P	P	I	S	K	R	E	F	E	S
T	■	O	■	E	■	S	■	E	■	S
N	E	N	D	R	A	E	E	R	P	A
S	■	T	■	O	■	O	■	R	■	E
O	U	R	L	C	E	R	O	O	I	P
C	■	S	■	E	■	O	■	N	■	M
S	P	E	C	T	A	T	R	C	H	A

1. A person who wins a tournament. __ __ __ __ __ __ __ __

2. A group of teams that play each other. __ __ __ __ __ __

3. A person who participates in sports. __ __ __ __ __ __ __

4. A person who watches a match. __ __ __ __ __ __ __ __ __

5. A person you compete against. __ __ __ __ __ __ __ __

6. A place where tennis or basketball is played. __ __ __ __ __

7. An athlete who doesn't get paid for playing. __ __ __ __ __ __

8. A person who calls fouls in a game. __ __ __ __ __ __ __

9. Throw the ball to a teammate. __ __ __ __

10. A place where baseball or soccer is played. __ __ __ __ __ __ __

11. The opposite of offense. __ __ __ __ __ __ __

12. The best score or time ever. __ __ __ __ __ __

Hidden message: A sports phrase *Use the remaining letters from puzzle 7·7 to uncover a phrase related to sportsmanship.*

One reason sportsmanship is important:

__ __ __ __ __ __   __ __ __ __ __   __ __   __ __ __ __   __ __ __ __ __

Weather

VOCABULARY

below zero	drizzle	humid	shower
blizzard	flurries	lightning	sizzling
boiling hot	fog	minus ten	sleet
breeze	freezing cold	mist	snow
calm	frost	overcast	sunny
chilly	gale	partly cloudy	sunshine
clear	gusts	rain	thunder
downpour	hail	scorching	windy

PUZZLE 8·1

Definition match up: Types of weather *Match the following definitions with the previous vocabulary words.*

1. The opposite of windy _____

2. Short strong rushes of wind _____

3. A mixture of ice and rain _____

4. Sunshine mixed with clouds _____

5. A light wind _____

6. A cloud on ground level _____

7. A brief rainfall _____

8. Ice that forms on windows _____

9. A light rain _____

10. Another word for cloudy _____

11. Light snow with wind _____

12. A very strong wind _____

13. A heavy rainfall _____

14. High moisture content in the air _____

Lists: Weather words *Make lists under the following headings using the words from the vocabulary list. You can use a word more than once if you want.*

FORMS OF PRECIPITATION

_____

_____

_____

CLOUDY WEATHER

_____

_____

FAIR WEATHER

_____

_____

POOR VISIBILITY WEATHER

_____

_____

_____

WIND DESCRIPTIONS

_____

_____

_____

LOW TEMPERATURES

_____

_____

HIGH TEMPERATURES

_____

_____

INCLEMENT WEATHER

_____

_____

_____

Matching: Weather collocations *Match the following words with their collocations.*

below	gusts	partly	ultraviolet (uv)
boiling	inclement	poor	weather
freezing	minus	scattered	wind chill

1. _____ cloudy

2. _____ zero

3. _____ showers

4. _____ factor

5. _____ weather

6. _____ of wind

7. _____ rays

8. _____ hot

9. _____ cold

10. _____ twenty

11. _____ forecast

12. _____ visibility

Fill in the blanks: The weather *Complete the following paragraphs by filling in the blanks using the words provided.*

Predicting the weather

| decisions | hand | outside | temperatures |
| forecast | meteorologists | precipitation | |

Almost every newspaper or news show on TV provides its audience with a weather _____, which is a prediction of future weather. Knowing the weather helps people make _____ in their daily lives. If the forecast says there is a high chance of _____, then you know you should bring an umbrella when you go somewhere. On the other _____, if the forecast is for low _____, you know you should dress warm if you are going _____. People who make weather forecasts are called _____.

The water cycle

| atmosphere | condenses | force | runoff |
| clouds | evaporate | frigid | vapor |

The sun is the driving _____ behind much of the weather. On hot days, the sun heats up water in lakes and oceans causing it to _____. As it rises into the air, the water _____ cools off and _____ into droplets of water. If it is really _____, ice crystals will form instead. The droplets or crystals form _____ and eventually they become too heavy to stay in the _____, so they fall to the earth as precipitation. The water then flows back to the lakes and oceans as _____.

Weather forecast 1

| clear | high | overcast | percent |
| cool | humid | partly | up |

Today's weather is going to be hot and _____ with a _____ of 33 degrees Celsius. There will be lots of sunshine with _____ skies all morning followed by _____ cloudy skies in the afternoon. By evening, thunder clouds will roll in and there is a 70 _____ chance of rain by nightfall. Tomorrow, the weather will _____ off with maximum temperatures expected to reach 27 degrees Celsius. There will be _____ skies for most of the morning, but things should clear _____ by afternoon.

Weather forecast 2

abate	batter	gale	lows
advised	drop	gusts	severe

Most of today will be calm with _____ of wind picking up in the afternoon. However, there is a _____ weather warning in effect for the evening. _____ force winds are expected to _____ the coast well into the night. Residents are _____ to take precautions. As the heavy winds _____, you can expect a sudden _____ in temperature by morning with _____ of minus five.

Weather forecast 3

chains   elevations   expected   forecast   passes   subside

There is a 90 percent chance of rain in the _____ for tomorrow with snow predicted at higher _____. The precipitation is _____ to last well into the afternoon but eventually _____ sometime in the early evening. Motorists driving through mountain _____ are advised to carry _____ for their tires.

PUZZLE 8·5

Word search: Weather *Find the following words in the grid.*

```
T B L I Z Z A R D F R E E Z I N G C O L D E V R
O A T M O S P H E R E Z N Y L B E L O W Z E R O
R F C G H A I L A K G I W B O I L I N G H O T V
N C P R E C I P I T A T I O N S G A I R M A S S
A A F P A L V L V R E Y C Z H T U H U M I D V H
D L F P T E C N M Z S B B O F R O N T Q G P G Z
O M O F W A M I N U S T E N L Y F J N N I N R P
V A R L A R O V E R C A S T A D H E N Y I H C A
Z S E U V M E T E O R O L O G I S T Z L B N F N
H H C R E P A R T L Y C L O U D Y P Z N U K G B
M U A R I D G P R E D I C T I O N Z E Z G R N W
D R S I P O S L E E T A N G D R I Z Z L E Z J V
C R T E F W H S F R O S T U T S C Y R Q L T N C
H I A S Z N O U G I J B F S U N S H I N E W O N
I C R S Z P W X I A J I I T H E R M O M E T E R
L A I N S O E Y B Z L M Z S C O R C H I N G E U
L N D O D U R T E M P E R A T U R E M K O Z E B
Y E T W B R E E Z E L W T H U N D E R S I F Q H
```

Air mass	Drizzle	Humid	Scorching
Arid	Flurries	Hurricane	Shower
Atmosphere	Fog	Lightning	Sizzling
Below zero	Forecast	Meteorologist	Sleet
Blizzard	Freezing cold	Minus ten	Snow
Boiling hot	Front	Mist	Sunny
Breeze	Frost	Overcast	Sunshine
Calm	Gale	Partly cloudy	Temperature
Chilly	Gusts	Precipitation	Thermometer
Clear	Hail	Prediction	Thunder
Cold spell	Heat wave	Rain	Tornado
Downpour			

Crossword

Across

5. Another way to say cold.

6. Another way to say sunlight.

8. A light rain. Hint: It begins with D.

9. A time when too little rain causes rivers to dry up and plants to die.

12. Crystals of ice that fall from the sky.

13. Short strong winds: _____ of wind. Hint: It begins with G.

15. A mix of clouds and sunshine: _____ cloudy.

17. A light wind.

19. A cloud that sits on the ground.

21. The opposite of windy.

22. A prediction of future weather.

24. Any form of water that falls from the sky.

25. A person who studies the weather.

28. A dangerous twisting column of air.

29. Good weather for flying kites.

30. A very large and dangerous storm that brings strong winds and heavy rains.

31. Water that falls from the sky.

Down

1. A form of weather that can block the sun.

2. The amount of water vapor in the air. Hint: It begins with H.

3. A time when too much rain causes rivers to overflow.

4. A mixture of rain and snow.

7. The temperature at which water freezes (in Celsius).

10. Something people use when it rains.

11. Small, hard balls of ice that fall from the sky.

12. A piece of snow.

14. A tool used to measure temperature.

16. Flashes of light in a stormy sky.

17. Minus temperatures (in Celsius): _____ zero.

18. Another word for wet.

20. How hot or cold something is.

21. Not a cloud in the sky: A _____ day.

23. Another way to say cloudy.

26. A short rain.

27. The opposite of hot.

Idiom puzzle: Weather idioms *Complete the following weather-related idioms. Use the shape symbols below the blanks to help you solve the missing spaces.*

1. No matter what:

COME RAIN OR __ __ __ __ __ __
● 9 36 ♠ 23

2. Feeling sick:

UNDER THE __ __ __ __ __ __ __
8 ♣   ★ 20   41

3. Something completely unexpected:

A __ __ __ __ __ FROM THE BLUE
▲ 9 Ω ★

4. A friend only during the good times:

A __ __ __ __ __ __ - __ __ __ __ __ __ __ FRIEND
■   21 ◐ 25   6 30 ⊡ ♣ ◑

5. Feeling depressed:

__ __ __ __ __ IN THE DOLDRUMS
♦ ▼ Σ 22

6. Experience difficulties:

HIT __ __ __ __ __ __ WEATHER
◑ ▼ 40 ♥ 5

7. Very happy:

ON __ __ __ __ __ __ NINE
Ω ▼ 17 ♦

8. Be unrealistic or impractical:

HAVE YOUR __ __ __ __ __ IN THE CLOUDS
14 ♣ 32 ♦

9. Take a risk:

THROW CAUTION TO THE __ __ __ __ __
Σ 33 18 ♦

10. Try to do something impossible:

CHASE __ __ __ __ __ __ __ __ __
◑ 2 △ 34 ▲ ▼ Σ 35

11. Survive a crisis:

WEATHER A __ __ __ __ __ __ __
24 ★ ▼ ◑ 1

12. A downpour:

RAINING CATS AND __ __ __ __ __
♦ ▼ ♥ 6

13. Have no idea:

HAVEN'T THE __ __ __ __ __ __ __ __ __
■ ▼ ♥ ♥ 10   42 ★

14. Casually chat with someone:

SHOOT THE __ __ __ __ __ __ __
▲ ◐ ♣ 12   27

15. Very quick:

__ __ __ __ __ __ __ __ __ __ FAST
11 △ ♥ ⊡ 37 ♠ 29 ♠ ♥

16. Put money away for an emergency:

SAVE FOR A __ __ __ __ __ DAY
◐   28 7

17. A big fuss over a small problem:

A __ __ __ __ __ __ __ IN A TEAPOT
★ 15   38 ♣ ● 13

18. Something that brings happiness:

A RAY OF __ __ __ __ __ __ __ __
19   ♠ ● 26 △ ♠ 4

19. Get to know someone:

__ __ __ __ __ __ THE ICE
▲ 31 ♣   3

Code breaker: Weather proverbs *Use the number code from puzzle 8·7 to solve the following proverbs.*

1. *Take advantage of an opportunity while you have the chance:*

__ __ __ __   __ __ __   __ __ __ __ __   __ __ __   __ __ __   __ __ __ __ __ __
1 2 3 4   5 6 7   8 9 10 11 12   13 14 15   16 17 18   19 20 21 22 23 24

2. *Bad luck comes all at once:*

__ __ __ __   __ __   __ __ __ __ __,   __ __   __ __ __ __ __
25 26 27 28   29 30   31 32 33 34 35   36 37   38 39 40 41 42

VOCABULARY

advisory	cold front	gale force winds	sunburn
alert	cold spell	heatstroke	thermometer
anemometer	dehydration	heat wave	tornado
atmosphere	drought	hurricane	warm front
barometer	flood	hypothermia	warning
blizzard	frostbite	meteorologist	windchill factor

Definition match up: Types of weather *Match the definitions below with the vocabulary words above.*

1. Water covering the ground _____

2. A massive tropical storm _____

3. A person who forecasts weather _____

4. A time when the body overheats _____

5. Strong winds _____

6. A tool used to measure air pressure _____

7. A twisting column of air _____

8. A period of cold weather _____

9. A period of hot weather _____

10. A long period without rain _____

11. Injury due to extreme cold _____

12. How much colder the weather feels due to the wind _____

Lists: Extreme weather words *Make lists under the following headings using the words from the vocabulary box. You can use a word more than once if you want.*

DANGEROUS WEATHER-RELATED
HEALTH CONDITIONS

_____

_____

_____

_____

EXTREME WIND CONDITIONS

_____

_____

_____

TOOLS USED BY METEOROLOGISTS

_____

_____

_____

EXTREME TEMPERATURES

_____

_____

_____

NOTICES ISSUED WHEN EXTREME
WEATHER IS IN THE FORECAST

_____

_____

_____

TIMES WHEN THERE IS TOO LITTLE
OR TOO MUCH PRECIPITATION

_____

_____

_____

Fill in the blanks: Extreme weather *Complete the following paragraphs by filling in the blanks using the words provided.*

Extreme winds: The Beaufort scale

advisories	calm	force	life
breeze	damage	hurricanes	scale

Extreme wind conditions cause billions of dollars in _____ around the world every year. To help mitigate damage and loss of _____, meteorologists issue weather _____ whenever storms are in the forecast. They use the Beaufort _____ to rank the severity of wind. A _____ day with no wind is a zero on this scale. A gentle _____ is a three. Gale _____ winds start at eight on this scale and the most dangerous storms, called _____, are a twelve.

Extreme cold

amputation	core	fingers	frostbite
consequences	dress	frigid	hypothermia

When you have to go out into extremely _____ temperatures, it is important to

_____ for the weather. If you don't, the _____ can be deadly. Exposed

parts of the body can be affected by a condition known as _____, which is where

tissues in your body become frozen. In severe cases, this condition can result in the _____

of body parts such as _____ and toes. Another deadly condition caused by cold

temperatures is _____, which is where your _____ body temperature

drops to a dangerous level.

Extreme heat

colored	period	radiation	stroke
dehydration	perspiration	strenuous	wave

A heat _____ is when unusually high temperatures exist in a region for a

_____ of time. During heat waves, people are at risk of coming down with

heat _____, which results from overheating the body. To avoid this condition, you

should wear a wide-brimmed hat to block the sun's _____ and wear light-

_____ clothing that allows you to cool off through _____. It is also

important to drink plenty of liquids to prevent _____. Finally, you should avoid

_____ exercise.

Extreme precipitation

bridges	impassable	precipitation	wither
drought	overflow	submerge	

Too much or too little _____ can result in devastation for the people of a

region. Too much rain can cause flooding as rivers _____ their banks. Floods

wash away _____ and _____ roads and buildings under

water. Too much snow can also bury roads making them _____. Too little rain

can cause a _____ where crops _____ and brush fires

spread.

Crossword

Across

5. A period of unusually cold weather:
Cold _____.

6. Rain, snow, sleet, or hail.

8. The layer of air around Earth.

9. _____ lines were
knocked down during the storm.

10. A serious condition where exposed
tissues in your body freeze.

11. A tool used to measure temperature.

Down

1. _____ wither
during a drought.

2. A period of unusually hot weather:
Heat _____.

3. How hot or cold something is.

4. A person who forecasts the weather.

7. Water pipes _____
during the cold spell.

10. A prediction of the weather.

Across (cont.)

15. How much colder something is because of the wind: Wind _____ factor.

16. A dangerous twisting column of air.

18. A prolonged period of too little rainfall.

21. An extremely severe storm that causes widespread damage. Hint: It begins with H.

22. A serious condition where your body overheats: Heat _____.

23. A severe snowstorm.

24. Trees were _____ during the storm. Hint: It beings with U.

Down (cont.)

12. A serious condition where your body lacks water.

13. A serious condition where your body temperature drops to a dangerous level. Hint: It begins with H.

14. A time when rivers overflow.

17. A warning issued by the government when severe weather is approaching.

19. Strong winds.

20. A painful red skin condition from overexposure to the sun.

Climate

VOCABULARY		
alpine	fauna	prevailing wind
Antarctic	flora	rain forest
Arctic	humid	rain shadow
arid	insolation	taiga
cactus	monsoon	temperate regions
climate	ocean current	tropical regions
coniferous	permafrost	tundra
deciduous	polar regions	wetland
desert	prairie/steppe	
equator	precipitation	

PUZZLE
9·1

Word list: Climate *The words in the vocabulary box above are all related to climate. Look up any of the words you don't know and then match the words with the definitions to the right.*

1. The average weather in a region over a prolonged period of time _____

2. Very dry air _____

3. Very moist air _____

4. An arid region with sparse vegetation _____

5. The animals in a region _____

6. The vegetation in a region _____

7. A line that runs around the middle of the Earth _____

8. A cold treeless region in the Arctic _____

9. A tree adapted to desert regions _____

10. Trees with needles and cones _____

11. Trees that lose their leaves in autumn _____

12. The average wind direction in a region _____

13. A seasonal wind that brings rain in some parts of the world _____

14. The movement of water in the ocean _____

15. Ground that is permanently frozen _____

16. A cold northern forest _____

17. A forest with heavy annual precipitation _____

18. Regions that get enough precipitation for grasses to grow but not enough for forests _____
_____

19. The regions between the polar and tropical regions _____

20. The amount of the sun's radiation that hits a region _____

Labeling: Climate *Attach the climate-related labels to the following lists of words.*

cold climate biomes   geographical zones   living organisms in a region
factors that affect climate   grassland biomes   types of trees

1. _____

   taiga
   tundra

2. _____

   prairie/savanna
   steppe

3. _____

   insolation/ocean currents
   prevailing winds

4. _____

   polar/temperate
   tropical

5. _____

   flora
   fauna

6. _____

   coniferous
   deciduous

Matching: Climate collocations Match the climate words in the box with their collocations.

annual   coniferous   flora   prevailing   rain   tropical

1. _____ regions

2. _____ shadow

3. _____ winds

4. _____ rainfall

5. _____ tree

6. _____ and fauna

Fill in the blanks: Climate and weather *Complete the following paragraphs by filling in the blanks using the words provided.*

Climate

average	fauna	minimal	seasonal	temperature
dry	grasses	prevailing	support	

Climate is the _____ weather of an area over a prolonged period of time. The average _____, the average annual precipitation, and the _____ winds are all used to describe climate. Different climates support different flora and _____. For example, regions with _____ precipitation tend to be barren. Regions with a modest amount of precipitation can support _____ and other small plants. Regions with abundant precipitation will _____ forests of tall trees. Different regions have different _____ variations in climate. For example, in some regions there are four seasons: spring, summer, fall, and winter. In other regions, there is a wet and a _____ season.

Factors that affect climate

affects	factors	milder	shadow	wind
continents	insolation	mountain	tropical	

There are several _____ that affect climate. One factor is _____, or the amount of the sun's radiation that hits an area. _____ regions receive more radiation per area than polar regions, so they tend to have a much higher average temperature. Another factor that _____ climate is nearness to large bodies of water. Regions that are in the middle of _____ tend to have more extreme weather than regions near the coasts, where the climate tends to be much _____. _____ ranges can also affect climate by altering _____ and rain patterns. For example, there is often a rain _____ on the leeward side of mountain ranges.

Deserts and rain forests

abundant	arid	floor	precipitation
adapt	cacti	flora	sunlight

Deserts are _____ regions that receive very little annual _____. The _____ and fauna of desert regions have to _____ to the extreme conditions of life without water. For example, _____ are plants that have thick waxy stems that help them store water. Rain forests, on the other hand, receive _____ rainfall throughout the year. In rain forests, trees and plants compete so fiercely for space and _____ that very little light actually reaches the forest _____.

Polar regions

Arctic	coniferous	radiation	taiga
barren	frigid	result	tundra

The polar regions in the _____ and Antarctic receive less solar _____ than any other region on Earth. As a _____, these regions are far more _____. The far northern region of the world consists mostly of a _____, treeless biome called _____. South of this region are the cold northern forests, or _____, which are mostly composed of _____ trees.

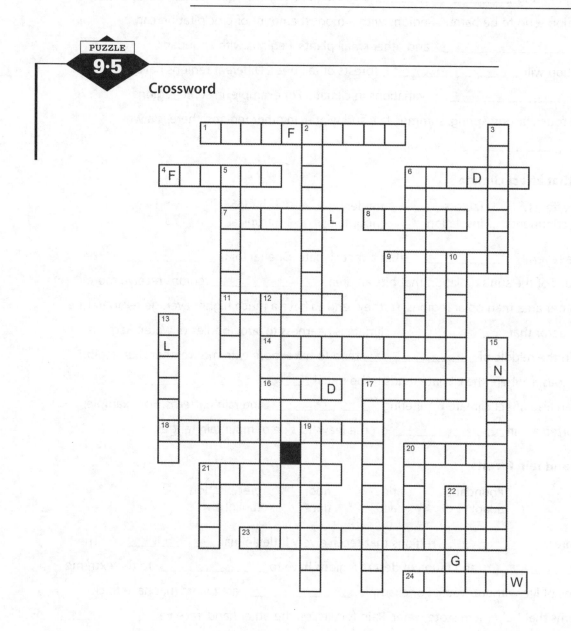

PUZZLE
9·5

Crossword

94 PRACTICE MAKES PERFECT English Vocabulary Games

Across

1. Trees that have needles and cones: _____ trees.

4. Another word for cold.

6. A cold, treeless area near the North Pole.

7. Another word for yearly.

8. Another way to say wet.

9. A dry, barren biome.

11. A high elevation biome.

14. A biome that receives abundant rainfall and supports dense forests.

16. Another way to say dry.

17. The regions near the poles.

18. How hot or cold something is.

20. The animals found in a region.

21. A wind that brings heavy rainfall in Southern Asia.

23. Rain, snow, sleet, or hail.

24. An area on the leeward side of a mountain range that receives little rainfall: Rain _____.

Down

2. How high up something is.

3. A flow of water in the ocean.

5. Steppe, prairie, or savanna.

6. The regions between the tropical and polar regions: _____ regions.

10. A line that runs around the middle of the Earth.

12. Ground that is frozen all year-round.

13. The average weather of a region over a long period of time.

15. The amount of solar radiation per area that reaches the Earth.

17. The average winds of a region: _____ winds.

19. The regions near the equator: _____ regions.

20. The plants found in a region.

21. The opposite of extreme (when talking about climate).

22. A cold northern forest composed mostly of coniferous trees.

Word search: Climate *Find the following words in the grid.*

```
G I L H E T D B V B O C E A N C U R R E N T X C
F X Q K S I J T R O P I C A L R L G S Z V C V A
I G P E R M A F R O S T P A K R I I G D Z M U K
G G R A I N S H A D O W N I K L C Q M X Y N R O
R A I N F O R E S T D N H B X S O P R A I R I E
I N S O L A T I O N A W F Q M Y N T D B T R Q A
J T E Q U A T O R V R J A S W E T L A N D E U K
J A R N T J Q B A F N F U C Q R I F B N D O C E
T I T O M O N S O O N O N D A D N C J A L L H X
G G R A S S L A N D R V A L A E E A N G W V C E
A A H H U M I D I E A I O R U R N C U W J C T N
L E X Q V S B Z F S B P D A Z A T T I E Y A W E
P L F S H V N I R E N N Q M G R A U J D R I E P
I P L I S Q N D Z R U E F T S C L S M E U Y S Z
N P O D X O I F E T W P A S S T E P P E D O Y O
E P R E C I P I T A T I O N W I B M X B M V U U
V U A X N C S R A I N F A L L C E L G K U K G S
V P R E V A I L I N G W I N D T C O A S T A L M
```

Alpine	Fauna	Prevailing wind
Arctic	Flora	Rain shadow
Arid	Grassland	Rainfall
Cactus	Humid	Rain forest
Climate	Insolation	Savanna
Coastal	Monsoon	Steppe
Coniferous	Ocean current	Taiga
Continental	Permafrost	Temperate
Deciduous	Polar	Tropical
Desert	Prairie	Tundra
Equator	Precipitation	Wetland

Clothing and fashion ·10·

VOCABULARY

alter	garment	overalls	skirt
blouse	(high) heels	pajamas	suit
coat	hoodie	pants	sweatshirt
cobbler	jacket	running shoes*	tailor
dress	mannequin	secondhand	tie
dye	mend	shirt	trend
fashion designer	model	shorts	vest

*regional variations include *sneakers, runners, trainers,* and *gym* or *athletic shoes.*

PUZZLE 10·1

Definition match up: Clothing *Match the following descriptions with words from the vocabulary list.*

1. Something popular now _____

2. Fix torn or ripped clothes _____

3. A sleeveless garment _____

4. A sweatshirt with a hood _____

5. Clothing that covers the body and legs _____

6. A person who sews clothes _____

7. Clothes worn on interviews _____

8. A person who displays new designs _____

9. Another word for used _____

10. Someone who makes/fixes shoes _____

11. An article of clothing _____

12. A loose shirt worn by women _____

13. Change the color of something _____

14. A dummy used to display clothes _____

15. Clothes you wear to bed _____

16. Someone who designs new lines of clothing _____

Labeling: Fashion vocabulary *Attach the label in the box to the following word lists.*

beachwear	eye wear	formal wear	undergarments	women's apparel
causal wear	footwear	protective wear	winter clothes	

1. _____

blouse
dress
skirt

2. _____

bikini
sun hat
swimsuit

3. _____

gloves
goggles
helmet

4. _____

suit and tie
evening gown
tuxedo

5. _____

jeans
shorts
T-shirt

6. _____

contacts
glasses
sunglasses

7. _____

boxers
bras
briefs

8. _____

boots
heels
sandals

9. _____

coat
mittens
scarf

animal print	floral/floral print	nylon	silk
argyle	formal	paisley	sleeveless
baggy	khaki	pastel	striped
beige	lavender	plaid	suede
bright	leather	plain/solid	tight
casual	light	polka dot	traditional
checked	long-sleeved	polyester	turquoise
cotton	loose	retro	turtleneck
dark	navy	rubber	tweed
denim	neon	short-sleeved	wool

PUZZLE 10·3

Word sort: Fashion trends *Sort the vocabulary words in the previous box into the following categories.*

COLOR/COLOR ADJECTIVE	PATTERN	MATERIAL	FIT/STYLE/OCCASION
_____	_____	_____	_____
_____	_____	_____	_____
_____	_____	_____	_____
_____	_____	_____	_____

PUZZLE 10·4

Labeling: Fashion vocabulary *Attach the label in the box to the following word lists.*

Compliments about clothes
Cosmetic/makeup
Fashion accessories

People working in the fashion industry
Places where fashion is displayed
Synonyms for clothes

Synonyms for fashionable
Things used to keep clothes in place
Ways to change clothes

1. _____

fashion show
mannequin
magazine

2. _____

apparel
attire
outfit

3. _____

It looks good on you.
It suits you.
It matches your hair.

4. _____

fashion designer
model
tailor

5. _____

    eye shadow
    lipstick
    nail polish

6. _____

    alter
    hem
    mend

7. _____

    handbag
    necklace
    ring

8. _____

    button
    zipper
    strap

9. _____

    in (style)
    stylish
    trendy

PUZZLE 10·5

Fill in the blanks: Fashion trends *Complete the following paragraphs by filling in the blanks using the words provided.*

Fashion trends

conscious   fads   fashion   in   novelty   retro   out   stylish   trend

Every season, the _____ industry works hard to design new lines of clothing. New fashions are constantly coming _____ style. People who wear the latest designs are said to be _____ or fashion-_____. When a new style is becoming popular, we call it a fashion _____. _____ are trends that spread quickly throughout society. Fads rarely last, however. Once the _____ wears off, many fashion designs go _____ of style. Though sometimes, old fashions come back in style and we call this a _____ look.

Fashion show

designs   magazine   models   photographers   runway   show

A good place to see upcoming fashion trends is a fashion _____, which is put on by designers to showcase their latest lines of clothing. There you will see _____ wearing the latest _____. The audience is often packed with _____ who take pictures of the models walking down the _____. If you can't make a fashion show, you can always flip through the pages of a fashion _____.

Shopping for clothes

catches   dressing   latest   mannequins   outfit   try   window

Another way to see what's in style is to go _____ shopping around the city. Shopkeepers put _____ wearing the _____ designs on display in their windows to give you an idea of how an _____ will look on you. However, if something _____ your eye, you should still _____ it on before you buy it. Most clothing stores have _____ rooms that allow you to do this.

Choosing the right clothes

fits   looks   match   suit   tight   uncomfortable

When you buy clothes, you want to find something that _____ you. If your clothes are too _____ or too loose, you will feel _____. You also want to find something that _____ good on you. When clothes go well together, we say that they _____. If the clothes fit your character, we say they _____ you.

Shopping on a budget

afford   into   online   prices   sale   secondhand   steep

Not everybody can _____ to pay for the latest fashions. Others simply aren't that _____ fashion. And so, some people go shopping at _____ clothing shops that sell used clothing for cheap _____. Other people prefer to shop _____ where they can get _____ discounts at the click of a mouse. Still others wait till a trend has passed and the clothes they want go on _____.

Word search: Fashion trends Find the following words in the grid.

```
G F L O R A L E O P A R D P R I N T X R X Q
H T Z A P H O T O G R A P H E R B A T H L A
S L E E V E L E S S E N W J N E R C B I U P
F O R M A L S B U B G A W O O L Z U U S D J
B M K P C N K I D X X V L G C V K V J V K W
L O Z K B B T E L J E Y C M A N N E Q U I N
N D G A X E P I Z K N C A S U A L Y F S P M
R E P A M I S P G H A R R A M A G A Z I N E
P L I L R G F A S H I O N S H O W J V D T Y
A E V T H E X S Z B T K F M D D T Y I I A E
I A S Y L P D T T W N H X R I I G A F W D I
S T Y L E O L E A P P A R E L G L T N E D S
L H R R A L P L N A U K A U A P U U U E X J
E E O E X K L N G I Z I Z B B O R S K O G X
Y R K T L A A C B W M O A B V B J C A R K M
C S V R X D I J X S H O R T S L E E V E D K
T P R O L O N G S L E E V E D H M R W L C I
T R A D I T I O N A L N K F C O T T O N A M
```

Apparel	Khaki	Paisley	Silk
Baggy	Leather	Pastel	Sleeveless
Beige	Leopard print	Photographer	Striped
Casual	Long-sleeved	Plaid	Style
Checked	Magazine	Plain	Tight
Cotton	Mannequin	Polka dot	Traditional
Denim	Model	Retro	Wool
Fashion show	Navy	Rubber	
Floral	Nylon	Runway	
Formal	Outfit	Short-sleeved	

Crossword

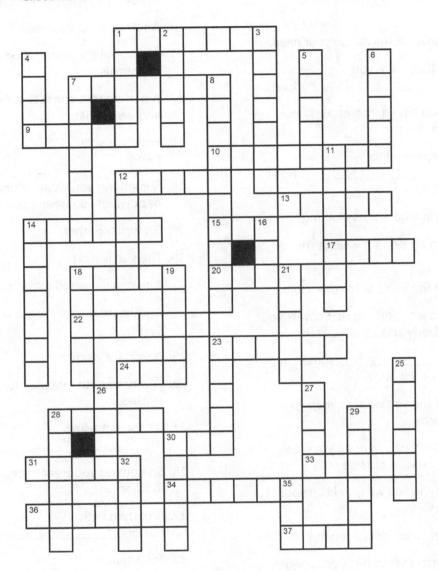

Across

1. Clothes you wear in bed.

7. Footwear for the beach.

9. An article of clothing that women wear instead of pants.

10. Pants that come up to and over your chest.

12. A pattern with just a solid color and no designs.

13. Something you wrap around your neck in winter.

Down

1. An article of clothing that covers your legs.

2. Pants made from denim.

3. A pattern with lines.

4. A compliment: Those pants look _____ on you!

5. A pattern with circles: _____ dot.

6. Footwear for hiking.

Across (cont.)

14. Type of clothes you wear to weddings, funerals, and job interviews.

15. Something you wear on your head.

17. Shoes that make you taller: _____ heels.

18. A person who demonstrates new fashions.

20. What you need to sew: _____ and thread.

22. A person who makes clothing.

23. Something women wear at the beach.

24. Something you use to color cloth.

28. An article of clothing that covers your upper body and arms.

30. _____ something on to see if it fits.

31. Something you wear to keep your feet warm.

33. Something you wear on your feet when you walk outside.

34. Something you wear to keep your hands warm.

36. Another word for fashionable.

37. A material that comes from sheep and is used to make sweaters.

Down (cont.)

7. Something you wear over your shirt to keep you warm in winter.

8. Another word for used.

11. A material that comes from the skin of animals.

12. A pattern that consists of horizontal and vertical lines.

14. What's in style: _____ trends.

16. Something you wear around your neck when you wear a suit.

18. Go well together.

19. The size is too big.

21. A material used to make jeans.

23. Another way to say loose (as in loose pants).

25. A shirt for women.

26. A very smooth material used to make clothes.

27. It's the right size: It _____.

28. Something you wear instead of pants in summer.

29. A pattern with flowers: _____ print.

30. Too small.

32. Something men wear at a job interview.

35. What you do to fix your clothes.

The arts: Performing arts and visual arts

Performing arts

VOCABULARY

actor	dancer	prop/scenery/set
applause	gesture	rehearsal
audience	illusion	rehearse
audition	instrument	score
ballet	magician	script
choreography	makeup	spontaneous
comedian	mime	spotlight
comedy	musical	stage
composer	musician	stand-up
conductor	opera	theater
costumes	performance	tragedy

PUZZLE

11·1

Word list: Performing arts *The words in the vocabulary box are related to the performing arts. Look up any of the words you don't know and then find a word from the box that could match each definition to the right.*

1. A person who performs in a play _____

2. A person who tell jokes on a stage _____

3. A person who writes music _____

4. A person who performs without making sound _____

5. A person who performs tricks and illusions _____

6. Something performers wear _____

7. People who see a performance _____

8. Clapping hands at the end of a performance _____

9. A document with an actor's lines on it _____

10. A play with many songs in it _____

11. Not planned _____

12. A bright light that shines on a performer _____

13. A building where plays are performed _____

14. A place in a building where plays are performed _____

15. Things on a stage _____

16. A type of comedian who tells jokes on a stage _____

17. A play that makes you laugh _____

18. A play with a sad ending _____

19. A trick where the audience is led to believe something that is not real _____

20. A type of dance _____

21. A written form of a musical composition _____

22. A hand motion or facial expression _____

23. The sequence of motions in a dance performance _____

Labeling: Performing arts *Attach the performing arts–related labels to the following lists of words.*

documents used by performers   performing artists   things performers wear
people who direct performers   things done at a rehearsal   types of plays

1. _____

musical
tragedy

2. _____

ballerina
musician

3. _____

go over lines
practice parts

4. _____

makeup
costumes

5. _____

score
script

6. _____

conductor
stage manager

Fill in the blanks: Performing arts *Complete the following paragraphs by filling in the blanks using the words provided.*

The performing arts

ballerinas	comedian	jokes	opera	stand-up
bodies	illusions	magic	performing	

Dance, theater, and _____ are all examples of traditional _____

arts. These are art forms where artists use their _____ and voice to create

art. When people think of performing arts, they often think of dancers such

as _____ or singers in a musical. However, there are many unusual forms of

performing arts as well, such as _____ comedy and _____

shows. In stand-up comedy, a _____ comes on stage and tries to make you

laugh by telling _____. In a magic show, a magician performs tricks

and _____ to amaze and entertain you.

Taking part in a musical

audience	cast	part	rehearsal	try
audition	memorize	putting	try	

Your school is _____ on a musical and you decide you would like

to _____ out for it. First, you will have to go to an _____

where you can demonstrate your singing and acting _____. If all goes well,

you will get the _____. Next, you will go to the first _____

where you will meet the rest of the _____. Over the coming weeks you will

have many more rehearsals and you will have to _____ your lines and perfect

your songs. Finally, on opening night you will perform in front of an _____.

The theater

actors	costumes	props	stage	tragedies
comedies	makeup	set	theater	

_____ is one of the oldest performing arts. In ancient Greece, theater was

divided into two types of plays: _____, which were meant to make you

laugh, and _____, which usually had an unhappy ending. Plays are performed

on a _____ by _____ wearing _____

and _____. The actors also use _____ such as swords to

make the play more convincing. And often, there is an elaborate _____ on

the stage as well.

Choreography

cheerleading   dance   fight   sequences   synchronized
choregraphy   fashion   gymnastics   skating

_____ is the art of coordinating and planning _____ of

movements. When most people think of choreography, they think of _____,

but choreography can be found in many other performing arts as well. For example,

choreography can be found in such diverse performances as _____ shows

and _____ at sports events. You can also see choreography in Olympic sports

such as _____, _____ swimming, and

ice _____. You can even see choreography in the _____

scenes of action movies.

Crossword

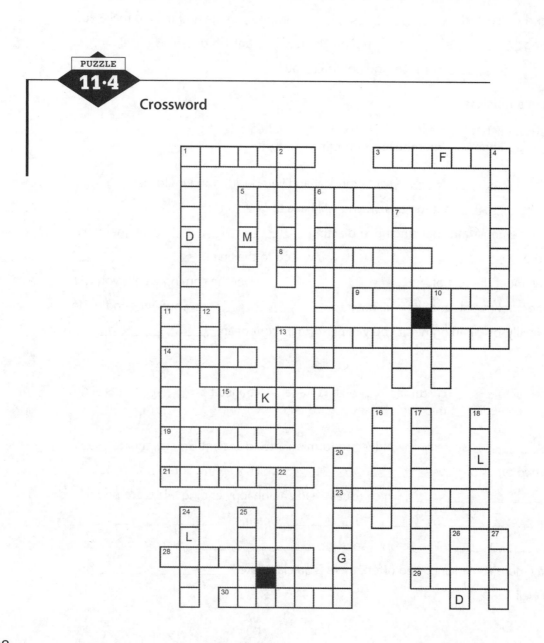

Across

1. What an actor wears.

3. Take part in a play or a show.

5. A person who plays an instrument.

8. A time when a person tries out for a part.

9. A magic trick that makes you believe something that is not real.

13. A sequence of coordinated dance moves.

14. A group of singers.

15. Something actors apply to their faces.

19. A play with an unhappy ending.

21. The people who watch a performance.

23. The clapping of hands by the audience.

28. Someone who writes music.

29. Something actors memorize.

30. A hand motion or facial expression.

Down

1. A person who tells humorous stories on a stage.

2. A play in which the actors sing many songs.

4. A person who performs magic tricks.

5. A performer who makes no sound and uses no props.

6. The person who leads an orchestra.

7. A bright light that is shone on performers.

10. A place in a building where performances are given.

11. A group of musicians (especially one that has winds, bass, strings, and percussion instruments).

12. Something an actor uses or holds on stage.

13. A play that makes you laugh.

16. A play written on paper.

17. A practice session for a play or concert.

18. A type of dance performance.

20. What actors say to each other.

22. A performance put on by musicians.

24. A type of circus performer.

25. Music that is written on paper.

26. A group of musicians.

27. Something you wear over your face.

Word search: Performing arts *Find the following words in the grid.*

```
W H A L A E P R L N R S E H M S P O T L I G H T
Y B H K H O J F O Y O H Q C O S T U M E C L X D
V R E D R J K I D E C F Z A K M A K C L M U S T
U H V P S P T E W B L V Q S M A U E Y G M U E R
Z L D E J I M O S I O G A X B A L S G L V R S C
E H T N D O T H K A W M J B P F K U I T F V U Y
X H R U C M O E R K N K D Y A O R E F C P R M E
C O A M G E S T U R E Q D I A L O G U E I M Y O
O K G P P M S N L P U T L S D N L D O P Q A M F
M P E I R E H E A R S A L Z X S P E P Y J R N T
P E D R H A R A J U C I B X W Y J W T S A Y I W
O R Y C F Y P N T I D L U G C O N D U C T O R W
S F R L M P I P S Y P I D G H I L L U S I O N S
E O U S J I I U C O N C E R T P K I Q U I A O F
R R B A C R M A G I C I A N H K Z N T S Z N G O
X M A R C O D E I Q U O T N C O M E D I A N V D
W H N S C H R S T G C H O I R E W S T A G E D J
C Q D C H O R E O G R A P H Y A P P L A U S E J
```

Applause	Concert	Musical
Audience	Conductor	Musician
Audition	Costume	Orchestra
Ballet	Dialogue	Perform
Band	Gesture	Prop
Choir	Illusion	Rehearsal
Choreography	Lines	Score
Clown	Magician	Script
Comedian	Makeup	Spotlight
Comedy	Mask	Stage
Composer	Mime	Tragedy

Idiom puzzle: Performing arts idioms *Complete the following performing arts–related idioms. Hint: You can use the shape symbols below the blanks to help you solve the puzzle.*

1. Brag or boast:

TOOT YOUR OWN _ _ _ _ _
♦ ★ 16 35

2. Face the consequences of your actions:

PAY THE _ _ _ _ _ _
1 ▼ 14 ♠ ♥

3. Very cheap:

FOR A _ _ _ _ _
30 ★ ♣ 32

4. Deception and trickery:

SMOKE AND _ _ _ _ _ _ _ _
Σ ▼ ♥ 2 33 ♥ △

5. The end of something:

THE FINAL _ _ _ _ _ _ _ _
◑ ⊡ ♥ 21 ● ▼ ♣

6. In good health:

FIT AS A _ _ _ _ _ _ _
17 ▼   ■ 23

7. "Good luck!": "

_ _ _ _ _ _ A LEG"
♥ 8 ● 11

8. Just what you wanted to hear:

_ _ _ _ _ TO YOUR EARS
28 ⊡ △ ▼ 7

9. Make a problem go away without any effort:

WAVE A _ _ _ _ _ _ WAND
9 ● Ω 6 ◐

10. So good that the next person will look bad:

A HARD _ _ _ _ TO FOLLOW
● ◑ 20

11. Be better than anyone else at an event:

STEAL THE _ _ _ _ _
△ 22 ★

12. The center of attention or public interest:

IN THE _ _ _ _ _ _ _ _ _
■ ▼ Σ ♠ ■ ▼ Ω ♦ 5

13. A very funny person:

A BARREL OF _ _ _ _ _ _ _
■ 10 ⊡ Ω 25 △

14. Out of the public view or in secret:

BEHIND THE _ _ _ _ _ _ _
24 ◐ ♠ ♣ 12 △

15. Distractions from real problems or issues:

BREAD AND _ _ _ _ _ _ _ _
◐ ▼ ♥ 19 ⊡ △ 18 △

16. Change your opinion or attitude:

CHANGE YOUR _ _ _ _ _
▲ 29 ♣ 15

17. Prepare for some activity:

SET THE _ _ _ _ _ _
13 31 ● Ω ♠

18. Both people share some blame for a dispute:

IT TAKES TWO TO _ _ _ _ _
▲ 3 ♣ Ω 26

19. A person who constantly jokes around:

THE CLASS _ _ _ _ _
4 ■ 34 27 ♣

Code breaker: Two proverbs *Use the number code from puzzle 10·6 to solve the two proverbs.*

1. *Why performers go to rehearsals:*

— — — — — — — —   — — — — —   — — — — — — —
1 2 3 4 5 6 7 8   9 10 11 12 13   14 15 16 17 18 19 20

2. *We must continue no matter what difficulties we face:*

— — —   — — — —   — — — —   — — —   — —
21 22 23   24 25 26 27   28 29 30 31   32 33   34 35

Visual arts

VOCABULARY

abstract	foreground	point of view
background	graffiti	portfolio
canvas	graphic design	portrait
carve/etch	handicraft	realistic
ceramics/pottery	hues	resemble
creativity/originality	illustrate/sketch	sculpture
decorative	image	shading
depict/portray	masterpiece	texture
design	mosaic	visual
distort	mural	vivid
exhibit/exhibition	perspective drawing	

Word list *The words in the box are related to the visual arts. Look up any of the words you don't know and then find a word that could match each definition to the right.*

1. Another way to say draw _____

2. Use a cutting tool to make a work of art _____

3. An outstanding work of art _____

4. That which can be seen _____

5. A showing of artwork to the public _____

6. A collection of an artist's work _____

7. The faraway area in a two-dimensional picture _____

8. The close-up area in a two-dimensional picture _____

9. A large painting done on a wall _____

10. An image created using small pieces of stone, tiles, paper, or glass _____

11. The angle at which something is viewed _____

12. The use of lines and shading to portray three-dimensional objects in two dimensions _____

_____

13. Art that closely resembles the objects it represents _____

14. Art that does not look at all like the objects it is meant to portray _____

15. Represent or show an object in a work of art _____

16. Three-dimensional works of art _____

17. How the surface of an object feels or appears _____

18. Using black and white to represent depth _____

19. The ability to think up new ideas _____

20. Another word for colors _____

21. Very bright (used to describe colors) _____

22. A picture of a person _____

PUZZLE
11·9

Labeling: Visual arts *Attach the visual arts–related labels to the following lists of words.*

drawings   methods of creating art   visual artists
elements of an artwork   places to view art   works of art

1. _____   4. _____

mosaic   exhibition
mural   gallery
sculpture   museum

2. _____   5. _____

animator   shape
illustrator   color
sculptor   texture

3. _____   6. _____

carve   doodles
draw   illustrations
etch   sketches

Fill in the blanks: Visual arts *Complete the following paragraphs by filling in the blanks using the words provided.*

The visual arts

appreciation	experience	practical	sculpture
creation	furniture	provocative	statement

Visual art is the _____ of images or objects through methods such as painting, _____, or photography. Some visual arts are meant to provide a pleasurable viewing _____. In this type of art, the artist might see beauty in a particular subject matter and wish to impart an _____ of that beauty to the viewer. Other visual arts are meant to be _____ and stimulate thought or debate among the viewers. In this type of artwork, the artist is trying to make a _____. Still other visual arts have a _____ purpose such as a painted bowl or a carved piece of _____.

Types of visual arts

canvas	metal	murals	sculpting
designers	mosaics	popularity	visual

Over the centuries, artists have developed many techniques for creating _____ arts. Traditionally, artists favored painting on _____ or _____ objects out of wood, _____, ivory, or stone. Some artists have created large paintings on walls called _____. Other artists have combined small pieces of tile or glass to create _____. However, many of these traditional techniques have lost _____ since the invention of computers. Today, many artists and _____ do much of their work sitting in front of a computer monitor.

Realism

converge	perspective	realistic	resembles	works
depth	posterity	Renaissance	technique	

When the depiction of an object in a work of art closely _____ the

actual object, we say that it is a _____ depiction of that object. From the

_____ to the 19th century, artists strived to improve their _____

so that they could create realistic _____ of art. Indeed, one function of art

in the past was the preservation of images for _____. One technique artists

employed was _____ drawing in which lines _____ to a point

on the horizon. This gives the impression of _____ on a two-dimensional

canvas.

Abstract art

abstract	experimenting	physical	shapes
emotions	invention	realism	view

Since the _____ of the camera, art has lost its function of preserving images for

posterity. Indeed, few artists can match the _____ of images taken by a camera.

Beginning in the 19th century, artists began _____ with new ways to represent

objects. These new works of art, called _____ art, were not realistic at all. For

example, Picasso painted portraits showing a person from two points of _____

at once. Other artists began painting things like ideas and _____, which have no

_____ reality whatsoever. In other words, these artists began using lines,

_____, and color to portray intangible things that cannot be seen or touched

at all.

Across

1. The place where near objects are located in a painting.

5. Cut wood or stone.

6. Art that is not realistic.

9. A work of art painted onto a wall.

11. A person who paints.

13. Another word for draw.

14. A type of drawing that creates the illusion of depth using converging lines.

Down

2. Art spray-painted onto buildings and subways.

3. Another way to say "Look similar."

4. Artwork shaped from stone or wood.

7. Art such as pottery that is made from clay.

8. The angle at which you see something: _____ of view.

10. Art that resembles the object being depicted.

Across (cont.)

15. That which can be seen.

16. Another word for draw.

21. Another word for portray.

23. An outstanding work of art.

24. A visual representation of something.

26. A work of art made from small pieces of tile, paper, glass, or stone.

27. An idea or work of art that hasn't been copied from somewhere else.

Down (cont.)

12. A material that many paintings are painted on.

17. A public showing of artwork.

18. Another word for color.

19. The place where faraway objects are located in a painting.

20. The ability to think up original ideas.

22. A collection of samples of an artist's work.

23. A place where artwork is displayed.

25. A person who creates works of art.

Word search: Visual arts *Find the following words in the grid.*

```
D I S T O R T I O N K T U K L N G P L H L L N Z
D E P I C T T R A D I T I O N A L O L A E O U L
K E H S C V W V F K U L V M S A I A N T I N R D
C E R A M I C S X M H T O K N T R O S T G O C S
B A C K G R O U N D U P E I I U I A I I T E A G
S P R D U S M E I G E R G F M T P B S P V I H M
C O P V N K A K F X U I F P A Q I E L I C Y C K
U R O D E J A B S T R A C T C H D U T I N U A W
L T R R E T C H C O R C N D X R C C A M Y E X O
P F T K T O N E G G I E B E H S E S E F L H V L
T O R N Q B T N S T S Y M C H P O A H Y A X L N
U L A J E I I B S E R X U O S M P O T T E R Y A
R I Y G H D J I R E Y E S R F S K S L I A X X M
E O A C A P L P L N P E E A C A N V A S V V E R
H M R H Z A E L T A L P U T E X T U R E V E F C
I A S U E R A E H S I T M I L L U S T R A T E J
J L I R D G I S V I N I U V G I W P A I N T E R
M A S T E R P I E C E E T E F O R E G R O U N D
```

Abstract	Gallery	Portfolio
Architecture	Graffiti	Portray
Background	Hue	Pottery
Canvas	Illustrate	Realistic
Carve	Image	Representational
Ceramics	Line	Sculptor
Creative	Masterpiece	Sculpture
Decorative	Mosaic	Shading
Depict	Mural	Shape
Design	Museum	Style
Distortion	Original	Texture
Etch	Painter	Tone
Exhibition	Pastel	Traditional
Foreground	Perspective	

Word paths: Visual arts *Find and circle the secret words below by following a connected path through the maze. Some words may overlap. Then use the remaining letters to uncover a proverb related to beauty.*

T	A	B	I	U	S	T	N	A	R	V
C	■	S	■	L	■	R	■	C	■	E
A	R	T	I	L	T	A	T	E	R	E
D	■	C	■	H	■	E	■	E	■	A
E	P	I	E	G	A	M	I	Y	E	L
V	■	O	■	F	■	T	■	C	■	I
I	S	U	S	E	U	H	H	I	T	S
O	■	A	■	E	■	B	■	E	■	E
R	H	L	M	U	R	A	L	O	L	C
I	■	A	■	D	■	E	■	R	■	E
G	I	N	M	A	S	T	E	R	P	I

1. A type of art you look at. __ __ __ __ __ __

2. A type of art that closely resembles an object. __ __ __ __ __ __ __ __ __

3. A type of art that doesn't resemble an object. __ __ __ __ __ __ __ __

4. Another word for draw. __ __ __ __ __ __ __ __ __ __

5. Another word for picture. __ __ __ __ __

6. Cut rock or wood. __ __ __ __ __

7. Another word for portray. __ __ __ __ __ __

8. An exceptional work of art. __ __ __ __ __ __ __ __ __ __ __

9. Not copied from somewhere else. __ __ __ __ __ __ __ __

10. A wall with a painting on it. __ __ __ __ __

11. Another word for colors. __ __ __ __

Hidden Message: A proverb about beauty: *Where beauty is located:*

__ __ __ __ __ __ __ __ __ __ __ __ __ __ __ __ __ __ __ __ __

Jobs and occupations

·12·

VOCABULARY

architect	curator	janitor	social worker
bank teller	editor	journalist	telemarketer
caterer	electrician	mechanic	trainer
civil servant	financial analyst	physician	weather forecaster
computer technician	guidance counselor	producer	web designer
construction worker	inspector	real estate agent	
consultant	interior designer	salesperson	
courier	interpreter	security guard	

PUZZLE 12·1

Word sort: Jobs *Match the following job descriptions with the job titles in the vocabulary box.*

1. Prepares food for events _____

2. Protects buildings from theft _____

3. Sells property for people _____

4. Designs buildings _____

5. Checks on quality _____

6. Works for the government _____

7. Helps people stay fit _____

8. Gives advice to students _____

9. Helps families with problems _____

10. Cleans buildings _____

11. Installs wires in buildings _____

12. Makes suggestion to writers _____

13. Treats sick or injured people _____

14. Delivers letters and parcels _____

15. Writes news articles _____

16. Fixes vehicles _____

17. Sells things over the phone _____

18. Advises companies _____

Labeling: Jobs and industries *Attach the field or industry label that follow to the lists of jobs.*

agriculture   health care   media
construction/trades hospitality   resource extraction
education   information technology (IT) tourism

1. _____

carpenter
electrician
plumber

2. _____

pharmacist
physician
therapist

3. _____

chef
front desk clerk
server/waiter

4. _____

network administrator
software engineer
web developer

5. _____

farmer
grower
rancher

6. _____

guide
travel agent
tour operator

7. _____

anchor
reporter
editor

8. _____

fisher
logger
miner

9. _____

instructor
principal
teacher

Word search: Jobs and occupations *Find the following words listed in the grid.*

```
S A L E S P E R S O N E W S A N C H O R E I D L
T N J R E A L E S T A T E A G E N T H D A S V T
O X O Q P L U M B E R C E L E C T R I C I A N K
C O U R I E R K Y D L U M Q L C J U R D Z A R T
K H R A N Z C T F H D H B A E B G O R I T O S N
B B N K T H J E M B Y G P T L R T A Z L L I A N
R A A M E C H A N I C I I R U A U S U E P I C G
O N L I R Z T C V G C H O O R G N S S A C J Y K
K K I C P W T H V N C S T U Y A N N R I U R E R
E T S L R R R E I R S W C T I O U E N M O F E J
R E T K E I E R A E T G I C C O H H R T K E O D
W L O X T T P F F L B R I A C T C R I Z N Q L A
S L M U E E O O O T U S M T C E T N E I C E I U
O E X I R R R Z D C Y I V M T T A W G W H J K E
J R R J N P T O E H H J K Q M J O N U R S E F B
E K T V M E E S P E C I V I L S E R V A N T L J
L O G G E R R A N F T X B W E B D E S I G N E R
P I L O T R I N S T R U C T O R E D I T O R O P
```

Actor	Interpreter	Real estate agent
Architect	Janitor	Reporter
Bank teller	Journalist	Salesperson
Chef	Logger	Security guard
Civil servant	Mechanic	Server
Consultant	Miner	Stockbroker
Counselor	News anchor	Teacher
Courier	Nurse	Technician
Curator	Physician	Therapist
Editor	Pilot	Tour guide
Electrician	Plumber	Web designer
Engineer	Principal	Writer
Instructor	Professor	

Crossword

Across

1. Someone who helps families deal with a crisis: _____ worker.

5. Somebody who raises sheep and cattle.

7. A person who takes you on tours: Tour _____.

9. A person who solves serious crimes.

10. A person who treats sick and injured people.

12. A person who fills cavities.

Down

1. A person who protects buildings from theft and vandalism: _____ guard.

2. A person who cooks in a fancy restaurant.

3. A person who cuts down trees.

4. A person who books flights and hotels for you: travel _____.

6. A person who designs buildings.

8. A person who fixes vehicles.

Across (cont.)

14. Someone who cleans buildings.

15. Someone who fixes sinks and toilets.

20. A person who makes sure buildings are safe: Building _____.

21. A person who sells houses: _____ _____ agent. (4, 6)

22. Someone who prepares foods for events.

24. A person who builds buildings: _____ worker.

25. A person who sells things over the phone.

10. A person who flies planes.

11. A person who advises businesses.

Down (cont.)

13. A person who works in a bank: Bank _____.

14. Somebody who writes news articles.

16. Someone who installs wires in houses.

17. Someone who digs metal ore from the Earth.

18. Somebody who tells you tomorrow's weather: Weather _____.

19. A person who grows crops.

22. A person who makes special deliveries to companies.

23. A person who works for the government: _____ servant.

Work life

·13·

VOCABULARY

Ways to end a job

be asked to leave
be dismissed
be given notice
be let go
be made redundant
get canned/sacked*

get fired
get laid off
leave your job
quit your job
resign
retire

*informal

PUZZLE

13·1

Word sort: Voluntary and involuntary reasons for leaving a job *If something is voluntary, it was your choice to do it. If something was involuntary, it was not your choice. Leaving your job is voluntary, but losing your job is involuntary. Find three phrases from the vocabulary box that refer to voluntary actions and three that refer to involuntary actions.*

VOLUNTARY   INVOLUNTARY

_____   _____

_____   _____

Find two phrases from the vocabulary box that are used to describe losing your job for poor work performance and two that describe losing your job for reasons beyond your control.

POOR WORK PERFORMANCE   REASONS BEYOND YOUR CONTROL

_____   _____

_____   _____

Matching: Job collocations *Match the following words with their collocations.*

| application | cover | dental | pleasant | sick | want |
| computer | dead-end | job | prospective | team | win-win |

1. _____ job
2. _____ letter
3. _____ interview
4. _____ literate
5. _____ player
6. _____ employer

7. _____ ad
8. _____ situation
9. _____ leave
10. _____ form
11. _____ plan
12. _____ demeanor

Fill in the blanks: Collocating prepositions *Fill in the blank with a collocating preposition.*

1. apply _____ a job

2. fill _____ an application form

3. get fired _____ a job

4. get fired _____ poor performance

5. graduate _____ a university

6. graduate _____ a field of study

7. prepare _____ an interview

8. work _____ a company

9. work _____ a field/profession

Fill in the blanks: Looking for work *Complete the following paragraphs by filling in the blanks using the words provided.*

Deciding to get a job

benefits	dissatisfied	graduated	loans	salary
challenge	fired	laid	looking	

There are many reasons why people might be _____ for work. Some have just

_____ from college, and they need to pay off student _____.

Other people might be _____ with their current job and are seeking something

that will _____ them more. Others might be after a higher _____

or better _____. Still others might have recently been _____ off

due to economic hard times. And some may have been _____ from their last

job for poor work performance.

Searching for jobs

bulletin	classified	Internet	mouth	résumé
centers	headhunter	listings	networking	

There are many places to find job _____. Many people check

the _____ ads in newspapers. Others visit the _____ boards

of college campuses and job _____. Still others use a _____,

which is a firm that specializes in locating highly skilled employees for companies. There are

also numerous job websites on the _____ where you can find job vacancies

or post your _____ for employers to look at. Another important source for

finding job vacancies is word of _____, which is why _____

is so important.

Finding the right job

compensation	health	long	paying	satisfaction
free	little	lower	plan	

Ideally, most people would like to have a high _____ job. But monetary

_____ is not the only thing to consider when looking for work. Job

_____ will determine how happy you are working in that position. It may be

worth settling for a _____ salary to do a job you love. Other benefits such as

_____ insurance or a dental _____ can end up saving you

thousands of dollars. Still other jobs can give you more _____ time to spend

with family and friends. That high-paying job might not be worth it if you have to work
_____ hours with _____ or no vacation.

Applying for and accepting a job

accept	apply	contract	interview	résumé
application	candidate	cover	offer	

Once you find the job you want, you have to _____ for the position. This can involve filling out an _____ form. For better jobs, you usually have to submit a _____ and a _____ letter. If an employer thinks you are a good _____ on paper, you might get a call asking you to come in for an _____. If that goes well, the employer will _____ you a position. If you _____ the company's offer, you usually sign a _____ and start working shortly thereafter.

Idiom puzzle: On the job *Complete the following job-related idioms. Use the shape symbols below the blanks to help you solve the missing spaces (the same symbol means the same letter).*

1. Be creative: THINK OUTSIDE THE __ __ __
                                    1 34

2. Put the blame on someone else: PASS THE __ __ __ __
                                          ★ 18 19 ♣

3. Do lots of work to get something: __ __ __ __ THROUGH HOOPS
                                       38 40

4. Get down to work: ROLL UP YOUR __ __ __ __ __ __ __
                                    ♠   24 ■ 28 ■ ♠

5. Make a good first impression: START OFF ON THE RIGHT __ __ __ __ __
                                                          9 32 3

6. Start all over again: START FROM __ __ __ __ __ __ __
                                     ♠ ◆ 10 30 12 ◆ 23

7. Undecided: ON THE __ __ __ __ __
                      6 ■ 35 22 ■

8. Decide to do something: MAKE UP YOUR __ __ __ __
                                         8 2 15 ♥

9. Help someone who is new: TAKE SOMEONE UNDER YOUR __ __ __ __
                                                      25   21 ●

10. Stop work and go home: CALL IT A __ __ __
                                      ♥ 20 36

11. Do something slowly: DRAG YOUR __ __ __ __
                                    7 44 ■ 33

12. Expensive: COST AN ARM AND A __ __ __
                                   31 29 ●

13. Be overwhelmed by a job: IN OVER YOUR __ __ __ __
                                           13 4 ♥

14. A new person's perspective: A FRESH PAIR OF __ __ __ __
                                                 11 16 ■ ♠

15. Ready to hear something: ALL __ __ __
                                  ■ 27 ♠

16. Time is running out: THE __ __ __ __ __ IS TICKING
                              ◆ 41 5 ◆ ♣

17. Share ideas with someone: PUT YOUR __ __ __ __ TOGETHER
                                        26 ■ 14 ♥ ♠

18. Teach a newbie what to do: SHOW SOMEONE THE __ __ __ __ __
                                                 39 17 ■ ♠

19. Cause problems: ROCK THE __ __ __ __
                              ★ 37 42 43

Code breaker: On the job *Use the number code in puzzle 13·5 to solve the following idioms.*

1. *Take on more work than you can handle:*

__ __ __ __ __ __ __ __ __ __ __ __ __ __ __ __ __ __ __ __ __ __ __ __ __
1 2 3 4   5 6 7   8 9 10 11   12 13 14 15   16 17 18   19 20 21   22 23 24 25

2. *Have a lot of work to do:*

__ __ __ __ __ __ __ __ __ __ __ __ __ __ __ __ __ __ __
26 27 28 29   30   31 32 33   34 35   36 37 38 39   40 41 42 43 44

Word paths: Jobs *Find and circle the secret words by following a connected path through the maze. Some words may overlap. Then use the remaining letters to uncover an idiom related to getting a job.*

O	C	I	P	S	U	M	S	A	L	A
N	■	N	■	E	■	E	■	C	■	R
T	U	T	E	R	L	G	L	R	A	Y
R	■	F	■	V	■	A	■	E	■	E
A	I	S	K	I	E	W	W	A	T	I
C	■	E	■	L	■	S	■	T	■	V
T	I	O	N	L	O	Y	E	R	R	E
O	■	I	■	P	■	I	■	N	■	A
M	G	S	E	M	T	I	Y	L	P	P
O	■	N	■	S	■	F	■	P		
R	P	E	B	E	N	E	T	I		

1. A document you submit when you apply. __ __ __ __ __ __

2. The money you earn in a month. __ __ __ __ __ __ __

3. The money you earn hourly. __ __ __ __ __

4. Submit an application for a job. __ __ __ __ __ __

5. Thinks outside the box. __ __ __ __ __ __ __ __ __

6. An increase in your pay. __ __ __ __ __ __

7. A document you sign when you accept an offer. __ __ __ __ __ __ __ __

8. (Get) a higher position in the company. __ __ __ __ __ __ __ __ __

9. Money you get when you retire. __ __ __ __ __ __ __ __

10. Someone who hires a worker. __ __ __ __ __ __ __ __ __

11. Something extra you get from a job. __ __ __ __ __ __ __ __

12. Something you are able to do. __ __ __ __ __ __

13. Money some employees earn for good service. __ __ __

14. A time when prospective employers ask questions. __ __ __ __ __ __ __ __ __ __

Hidden Message: Job idiom. *Use your connections to get someone a job.*

__ __ __ __ __   __   __ __ __ __   __ __ __ __ __ __ __

VOCABULARY

bonus	job satisfaction	skills
certificate	license	specialized knowledge
commissions	opportunities for promotion	tips
degree	pension	training
dental plan	proven track record	vacation
diploma	remuneration	volunteer experience
education	salary	wage
health insurance/medical plan	sick leave	work experience

PUZZLE

13·8

Definition match up: Looking for work *Match the following definitions with the words and phrases from the vocabulary box.*

1. Money you get when you retire _____

2. A monthly or yearly payment _____

3. Another word for compensation _____

4. An hourly or daily payment _____

5. Money you get for good service _____

6. Money you earn as a percentage of what you sell _____

PUZZLE

13·9

Word sort: Qualification and benefits *A qualification is something required for a job. A benefit is something you get from a job. Choose six words from the vocabulary box that are benefits and six that are qualifications and write them in the blanks.*

QUALIFICATIONS   BENEFITS

_____   _____

_____   _____

_____   _____

_____   _____

_____   _____

_____   _____

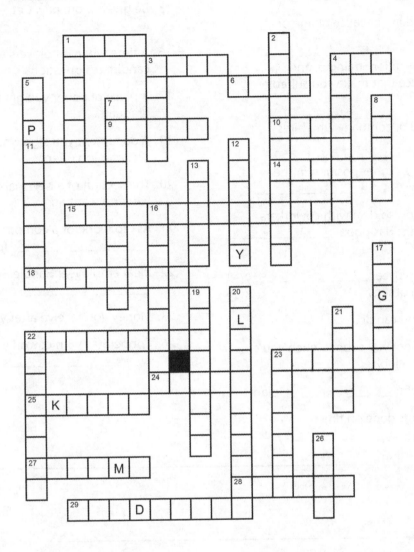

PUZZLE

13·10

Crossword

Across

1. Ideal job: _____ pay.

3. Lose your job due to economic hard times: Get _____ off.

4. Ideal employee: Thinks outside the _____.

6. Pay somebody to work for you: _____ someone.

9. A document you submit when you apply for a job: _____ letter.

10. Hourly pay.

Down

1. Job benefit: _____ insurance.

2. The opposite of lazy.

3. Time off when you are ill: Sick _____.

4. Things you get from a job beyond monetary compensation.

5. Have done a job in the past: Have work _____.

7. Another word for job.

8. Lose your job for poor work performance: Get _____.

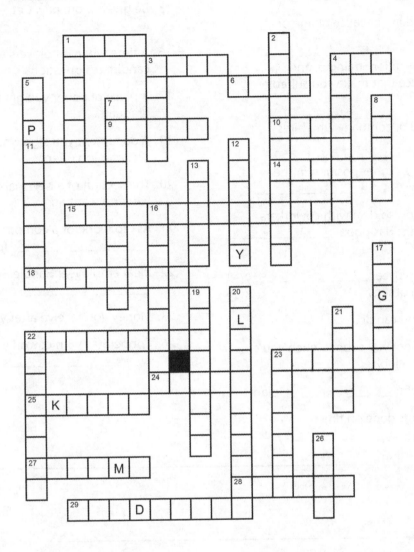

Across (cont.)

11. Hardworking: Has a good work _____.

14. Stop working because of age or health.

15. Skills, education, training, and experience that make you suitable for a job.

18. A person or company who hires people.

22. Be given a higher position in the company: Get a _____.

23. Knows how to deal with coworkers and clients: Has good _____ skills.

24. Ideal employee: _____ well with others.

25. Things you can do.

27. A document you submit when you apply for a job.

28. Job benefit: _____ plan.

29. Gets things done on time: Meets _____.

Down (cont.)

12. Monthly or yearly pay.

13. Be given more pay: Get a _____.

16. A time when employers ask job candidates questions.

17. A piece of paper you get when you graduate.

19. A document you sign when you accept a job offer.

20. The section of a newspaper where you find want ads.

21. Ask to work for a company: _____ for a job.

22. Ideal employee: Handles _____ well.

23. Money you receive after you retire.

26. Cooperates with coworkers: A _____ player.

PUZZLE

13·11

Fill in the blanks: The job interview *Complete the following paragraphs by filling in the blanks using the words provided.*

Quitting a dead-end job

anticipate	dissatisfied	interview	prospective
dead-end	dust	position	raise

Lately, you have been _____ with your job. You feel that you have gone as far as you can go in your current _____. You've asked for a _____, but the boss refused. You've asked for more responsibility, but again the boss refused. You are frustrated working in a low-paying job with no opportunities for advancement. In short, it's a _____ job. You've decided to find a new job. It's time to _____ off your resume and send it to _____ employers. When you do eventually get a call to come in for an _____, it's important to _____ and prepare for whatever questions prospective employers will ask you.

Reasons for changing jobs

<table>
<tr><td>advancement</td><td>mouth</td><td>positive</td><td>reasons</td></tr>
<tr><td>challenging</td><td>negative</td><td>problems</td><td>team</td></tr>
</table>

Some prospective employers might want to know your _____ for changing jobs. It is important that you avoid saying anything _____ about your current employer. People who are critical of their current employers are likely to bad-_____ prospective employers as well. Also, prospective employers will be worried that you are changing jobs because you have caused _____ at your current workplace. Employers want _____ players, not troublemakers. And so, it is important to find _____ reasons for wanting to change jobs, such as looking for something more _____ or finding work with more opportunities for _____.

Why work here?

costly   employers   goals   long-term   research   skills   stick   win-win

Other prospective _____ might ask you why you want to work at their company. Make sure you _____ the company well and have good reasons to want to work there. In particular, find out how your _____ can benefit the company and how the company's _____ match your own. You want to convince prospective employers that working for them will be a _____ situation. You also want to convince employers that you will be happy working there so that they are confident you will _____ around. Training new employees is _____ for companies, so they want people who will stay _____.

Your strengths and weaknesses

box   deadlines   ethic   honest   pressure   relevant   strengths

Prospective employers might also ask what your _____ and weaknesses are. It's important to make your strengths _____ to the job you are applying for. Try to think of concrete ways in which your strengths will help you do your job well. Strengths can include things such as your ability to work well under _____ or your ability to think outside the _____. You could also for example explain how your organizational skills and good work _____ allow you to constantly meet _____. As far as weaknesses go, be _____, but try to show how you've taken steps to overcome them.

Word search: The job interview *Find the following words listed in the grid.*

```
T C O M M I S S I O N E M A N E Y N N R
R H S R A A C O N T R A C T M N O O O D
A S I I N T E R V I E W I U M I I B E S
I F C A A J O B H K E U S R T T A E L E
N S K B G P B O S S Q E E O A L R I S E
I A L G E H P Y T N R T M S I G W O H K
N L E V R N N L O R T O N P E N S K I E
G A A T O A E I Y E R E S D L S C N F R
R R V I P L T F L P P O E K E O O O T O
E Y E M D A U R I M M G F N I I Y A M N
T Y O S P O E N O T A T I P S L C E O E
I C O U I V F C T W K S R N S S L P E O
R I C L O G T F H E U P E M P L O Y E R
E C E C B R N O T B E P A D I P L O M A
O P O S I T I O N W O R K Y R A I S E H
```

Apply	Employee	Occupation	Salary
Benefit	Employer	Pay	Seeker
Boss	Fire	Pension	Shift
Business	Firm	Position	Sick leave
Commission	Hire	Promotion	Skill
Company	Income	Quit	Tips
Compensation	Interview	Raise	Training
Contract	Job	Resign	Volunteer
Cover letter	Labor	Resume	Wage
Degree	Laid off	Retire	Work
Diploma	Manager		

Hidden messages: Contradicting proverbs
Once you have found all of the words, the remaining letters form two hidden proverbs that seem to contradict each other.

Proverb 1: __ __ __ __ __ __ __ __ __ __ __ __ __ __ __ __ __ __ __ __ __ __

Proverb 2: __ __ __ __ __ __ __ __ __ __ __ __ __ __ __ __ __ __ __ __

__ __ __ __ __

Word scramble: Job interview
Find the following words within the phrase "job interview." You can use the letters in any order, but you can only use each letter once.

JOB INTERVIEW

HINT: USE THE CODE BREAKER TO THE RIGHT TO HELP YOU SOLVE THE WORDS.

CLUES	ANSWERS	CODE BREAKER
1. A color	__ __ __ __ __	2 x x x 1
2. A planet's path	__ __ __ __ __	4 3 17 x 11
3. The opposite of exit	__ __ __ __ __	5 x 6 x x
4. A place that is smaller than a city	__ __ __ __	7 8 x
5. A hard metal	__ __ __ __	10 9 x x
6. A plant with a trunk	__ __ __ __	11 x x 12
7. A sibling born at the same time	__ __ __ __	31 8 x x
8. The opposite of always	__ __ __ __ __	13 x 14 x x
9. Ask someone to come over	__ __ __ __ __ __	15 x 16 x 11 x
10. Another word for steal	__ __ __	3 x 17
11. Choose your government	__ __ __ __	18 x 31 12
12. A part of your foot	__ __ __	20 x 19
13. Something electricity travels through	__ __ __ __	21 15 30 x
14. The past tense of go	__ __ __ __	8 x 22 20
15. Study something again	__ __ __ __ __ __	9 x 24 x x 23
16. A season	__ __ __ __ __	23 x x 6 x x
17. Numbers like 2, 4, 6, and 8	__ __ __ __	x 25 x 13
18. A short letter to someone	__ __ __ __	26 4 x x
19. An action word	__ __ __ __ __	18 x 3 2

20. A special happening   — — — — —   19 24 x 1 31

21. The opposite of lose   — — —   x 10 27

22. The type of cell that controls your body   — — — — —   22 5 x 25 x

23. Another word for wheel   — — — —   7 x 30 28

24. A place to bake bread   — — — —   29 14 x x

25. A hard tissue that supports your body   — — — —   17 29 26 x

26. Swear you will do something   — — —   16 x 8

27. An informal way to say adolescent   — — — —   11 x x 27

28. The opposite of old   — — —   x 28 21

Parts of the body

VOCABULARY

abdomen	eyelashes	jaw	ring
ankle	eyelid	joint	shin
back	eyes	knee	shoulder
belly button	fingers	knuckles	sole
calf	fist	lips	spine
cheek	foot	middle	temple
chest	forearm	nails	thigh
chin	forehead	neck	throat
earlobe	groin	nose	thumb
ears	heel	nostrils	toes
elbow	hip	palm	waist
eyebrow	index	pinky	wrist

PUZZLE
14·1

Definition match up: Parts of the body *Match the vocabulary words in the box with the following definitions.*

1. A common place on an ear to put earrings _____

2. A place where two bones are connected _____

3. The bottom of your foot _____

4. Your fingers and hand clenched together _____

5. The holes in your nose that you breathe through _____

6. The part of your face above your eyebrows _____

7. The joint that connects your hand and arm _____

8. The joint that connects your foot and leg _____

9. The back part of your foot _____

10. Your little finger _____

11. The upper part of your leg _____

12. The area above the hips _____.

141

13. A side of your face just below your eye _____

14. The flat area between your eye and upper ear _____

15. The finger you use to point _____

16. The lower part of your mouth _____

17. The part of your face under your lower lip _____

18. The strands of hair attached to your eyelids _____

19. The hair above your eyes and on your forehead _____

20. The area below your abdomen _____

21. The bottom part of your hand _____

22. The muscle at the back of your leg _____

PUZZLE
14·2

Word sort: Parts of the body *Find words from the vocabulary box to fill out the following word lists. Some words can fit in more than one list.*

PARTS OF YOUR FACE   JOINT LOCATIONS   FINGERS

_____   _____   _____

_____   _____   _____

_____   _____   _____

_____   _____   _____

_____   _____   _____

_____   _____   _____

_____

_____   PARTS OF A LEG   PARTS OF A FOOT

_____   _____   _____

_____   _____   _____

_____   _____   _____

Fill in the blanks: The human body *Complete the following paragraphs by filling in the blanks using the words provided.*

Your hands

gesturing	offensive	receptors	thumbs	wave
grasping	opposable	temperature	tools	

Human beings have two hands that are useful for _____ and holding objects.

One unique feature of the human hand is it has an _____ thumb, which allows

humans to manipulate _____. The fingers have very high concentrations of

nerve _____, which make the fingers very sensitive to _____

and touch. Human beings also use their hands for _____, which is a nonverbal

form of communication. For example, we _____ when we see people we

know. However, gestures have different meanings in different cultures. In North America,

a _____-up means that everything is OK, but in other cultures this gesture can

be highly _____.

Your face

cheeks	communication	face	frown	roll
chin	eyebrows	feel	question	smile

Your _____ is the front part of your head. It includes your eyes, nose, mouth,

_____ and _____. Like your hands, your face is important

for _____, especially letting others know how you _____. A wide

_____ can indicate that you are happy. A _____, on the other

hand, indicates you are not pleased. Raised _____ can communicate that you

are confused and would like to ask a _____. If you _____ your

eyes, it means you disapprove of what somebody has said.

Your legs

advantage	calf	erect	knee	sole
ankle	crawl	feet	shin	thigh

Except for infants, who _____, human beings almost always walk _____.

This gives humans the _____ of having their hands free to use tools. We walk on our

_____. The part of the foot that touches the ground is called the _____.

The foot is connected to the leg at the _____. Another joint, the _____,

connects the upper leg, called the _____, to the lower part of your leg where your

_____ and _____ are.

Abdomen and chest

abdomen	chest	intestines	organs	spine
belly	groin	lungs	shoulders	

Your abdomen and chest contain most of your internal _____. Your _____

contains your stomach and _____, whereas your _____ contains your

heart and _____. Your head and _____ are above your chest and

your _____ and legs are below your abdomen. Your _____ button is

right in the middle of your abdomen. Your _____ runs right down the center of

your back.

Crossword

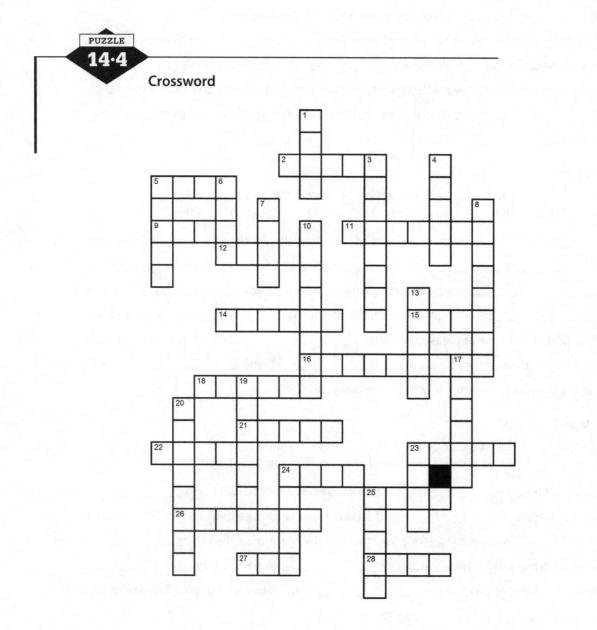

Across

2. A joint that connects the foot to the leg.

5. The muscle at the back of your lower leg.

9. The part of your body you use to hear.

11. The part of your body that contains your stomach and intestines.

12. Your upper leg.

14. The flat area on your head between your upper ear and your eye.

15. The back of your foot.

16. The strands of hair attached to your eyelids.

18. Index, middle, or pinky.

21. The front parts of your lower legs.

22. A joint that connects the hand to the arm.

23. Something that runs down the center of your back.

24. The part of your body you use to see.

25. The bottom of your hand.

26. A fleshy part of the ear that many people pierce.

27. The lower part of your mouth.

28. A joint that connects the upper and lower leg.

Down

1. The part of your body you use to grasp.

3. The hair above your eyes on the bottom part of the forehead.

4. The opposable finger.

5. A side of your face below your eye.

6. A hand with the fingers closed (clenched).

7. The area of your jaw below your lower lip.

8. Finger joints.

10. A joint that connects the arm to the body.

13. The part of your body that contains your heart and lungs.

17. Skin that covers an eye.

19. A hole in your nose that you breathe out of.

20. The part of your face above your eyebrows.

23. The bottom of your foot.

24. A joint that connects the forearm and upper arm.

25. Your smallest finger.

Word search: Parts of the body *Find the following words in the grid.*

```
N Y Z W V N W F O R E H E A D E B L B B P F K J
P C E E F A A B G W A I S T S E J H N N X E M I
E W U A J B Q I L R T H R O A T G E X Q J R K L
L E K K R Z H N L I Z Z B E L I M R Z R A D F C
O Y Y A V S H X S S V H D L H O N I O E Z D S Z
A E V E T E E W H T W W W T D B H C R I Y E I L
F L U D L D E N O Z H L K B P N O O C N N R V M
I A G C N I L M U U J Y A N A S F C H E S T E N
S S R I C H D L L R C G Q C E N O T E M P L E W
T H T B D H M T D P N U K N U C K L E S O M D B
H C A L F B I P E I N B H E Q K L E O K S J P
U J W T J X J N R R P A Q T E Y C E E I M B R D
M Q Q E O S P I N E A C W Y E Y E B R O W E O U
B Y E Z I E O I L X L K F S S H J S U R C C Y O
X N H G N B S B N H M B O M C H E E K J N K P L
K T I R T H J E O K P N O S T R I L S Z Z W P T
G Q P W A B O X H J Y K T W C F I N G E R S B L
E A R L O B E I V B E L L Y B U T T O N O U Q O
```

Abdomen	Eyebrow	Hip	Shin
Ankle	Eyelash	Jaw	Shoulder
Back	Eyelid	Joint	Sole
Belly button	Eyes	Knee	Spine
Calf	Fingers	Knuckles	Temple
Cheek	Fist	Nails	Thigh
Chest	Foot	Neck	Throat
Chin	Forearm	Nose	Thumb
Earlobe	Forehead	Nostrils	Toes
Ears	Groin	Palm	Waist
Elbow	Heel	Pinky	Wrist

Idiom puzzle: Body parts *Complete the following body part–related idioms. Use the shape symbols below the blanks to help you solve the missing spaces.*

1. Annoy someone: GET ON SOMEONE'S _ _ _ _ _ _
   10 ♦ ♣   ♦ ▲

2. (Say something) as loud as you can: AT THE TOP OF YOUR _ _ _ _ _
   ♠ ▼ 8 34 ▲

3. What you really want: YOUR _ _ _ _ _ _'_ DESIRE
   ◑ ♦ 28 15 22 ▲

4. Ask someone for ideas: PICK SOMEONE'S _ _ _ _ _
   14 ♣ 25 △ ●

5. Very quickly: IN THE _ _ _ _ _ OF AN EYE
   ★ ♠ 17 29 ♥

6. Space to move around: _ _ _ _ _ _ ROOM
   ♦ 32 ★ ⊡ 7

7. Offer to help someone if they help you: SCRATCH SOMEONE'S _ _ _ _ _
   ★ 9 19 ♥

8. Your fatal weakness: YOUR ACHILLES' _ _ _ _
   ◑ 33 ♦ 3

9. Get you angry: MAKE YOUR _ _ _ _ _ BOIL
   ★ ♠ ⊡ ⊡ 11

10. Can't express yourself: _ _ _ _ _ _ _ -TIED
    Ω 13 ●   ▼ ♦

11. Waiting eagerly to hear something: ALL _ _ _ _
    ♦ 1 5 ▲

12. A type of advertising: WORD OF _ _ _ _ _
    27 20 ▼ Ω ◑

13. A shocking secret: A _ _ _ _ _ _ _ _ _ IN THE CLOSET
    ▲ ♥ ♦ 2 ♦ Ω ⊡ 24

14. Argue about unimportant details: SPLIT _ _ _ _ _
    ◑ 16 △ 26 ▲

15. A person who annoys you: A PAIN IN THE _ _ _ _
    12 ♦   ♥

16. Stop worrying and relax: _ _ _ _ _ _ _ EASY
    4 ♣ ♦ 31 Ω ◑ ♦

17. Unable to speak: HAVE YOUR _ _ _ _ _ TIED
    ◑ 6 ● 30 21

18. Bother someone: GET UNDER SOMEONE'S _ _ _ _
    ▲ ♥ △ 18

19. Persuade someone to do something: TWIST SOMEONE'S _ _ _
    23 ♣

Code breaker: Two idioms *Use the number code in puzzle 14·6 to solve the following two body-related idioms.*

1. *Strong but not intelligent:*

— — —　— — — — —　— — — —　— — —　— — — — —
　1　2　3　　4　5　6　7　8　　9　10　11　　12　13　　14　15　16　17　18

2. *Very expensive:*

— — — —　— — —　— — — —　— — — —　— —　— — —
　19　20　21　22　　23　24　　25　26　27　　28　29　30　　31　　32　33　34

Common ailments

VOCABULARY

ache/pain	congestion	itchiness
allergies	constipation	pus
bite/sting	cough	rash
black eye	cut	runny nose
blister	diarrhea	scrape/scratch
blurred vision	dizziness	sore throat
broken bone	fever	sprained ankle
bruise	flu	stomachache
bump	headache/migraine	toothache
burn	heartburn/indigestion	vomiting
common cold	insomnia	

PUZZLE

15·1

Word list: Common ailments *Match the words in the vocabulary box with these definitions.*

1. A pain caused by a cavity in your mouth _____

2. Discomfort in the stomach from eating food _____

3. A pain in the stomach _____

4. Many small red bumps on the skin _____

5. Reactions to food, hair, or pollen (resulting in a congested nose or a rash on the skin) _____

6. An injury caused by touching hot objects _____

7. An injury caused by a sharp object such as a knife _____

8. What you do to clear congested or irritated lungs or throat _____

9. A swelling under the skin that comes from being hit by an object _____

_____

10. A common hiking injury where a person steps the wrong way and twists his or her foot _____

11. A common hiking injury caused by rubbing of a boot against the skin _____

12. Throwing up the contents of your stomach _____

13. Unable to focus or see clearly _____

14. A feeling that you are about to fall or briefly go unconscious (often accompanied by a dimmed vision) _____

15. The desire to scratch your skin _____

16. A raised body temperature _____

17. Loose, watery bowel movements _____

18. Difficulty having bowel movements _____

19. An injury that often requires a cast to keep the bone still while it mends _____

20. Purple or blue coloring under the skin _____

PUZZLE
15·2

Sorting: Injury versus illness Injuries *are instances of physical harm.* Illnesses *are caused by infections or by body organs not functioning properly. For each of the following categories, choose six words from the box that could be placed in each category.*

INJURIES

_____

_____

_____

_____

_____

_____

ILLNESSES

_____

_____

_____

_____

_____

_____

Fill in the blanks: Common ailments *Complete the following paragraphs by filling in the blanks using the words provided.*

Allergies

allergens	breathing	itchy	spring	trigger
allergies	immune	pollen	suffer	

People who _____ from allergies dread the coming of _____

because their _____ act up as the weather warms up. Many spring allergies are

caused by plant _____ that disperses in the wind. Some common symptoms of

allergies are _____, watery eyes and difficulty _____. An allergic

reaction is caused by a body's overactive _____ system attacking harmless

substances inside the body. Pollen is one of the most common _____, but many

other substances such as animal hair and dust can _____ an allergic reaction

as well.

The common cold

avoid	congestion	hands	sore	viral
caught	contagious	runny	symptoms	winter

Do you have a _____ nose, nasal _____, sneezing,

a _____ throat, or a headache? These are _____ of the

common cold. The common cold is a _____ infection of the upper respiratory

tract (your throat and nose). Colds can be _____ any time of the year but they

are most frequent during _____ and rainy weather. The common cold is

highly _____ and spreads quickly through schools and workplaces. To

prevent the common cold, you should _____ unnecessary contact with

people who have colds and wash your _____ frequently.

Injuries versus illnesses

confuse	flu	hurt	infections	sick	sprained	stubbed	wrong

Many students learning English _____ illnesses and injuries. Illnesses are

usually caused by _____ or by organs not functioning properly, whereas

injuries are usually caused by a physical process such as being hit by something or moving your

body the _____ way. The _____ and the common cold are

examples of illnesses and a _____ ankle or a _____ toe are

examples of injuries. When you have an illness, you say that you are _____,

but when you have an injury, you say that you are _____.

Skin ailments

ailments   burns   cuts   irritants   itchy   rash   relieve   skin   sunburns

The _____ is the organ that covers your body. There are many common _____ that affect the skin. A _____ is an area of red, raised spots on your skin. Rashes can be caused by allergies, skin _____, or even just something you ate. Rashes are often _____, but you should avoid scratching the affected area. There are many medicines on the market that can _____ the itchiness of a rash. Other common skin ailments include _____, which you get from touching something hot; _____ which you get from staying in the sun too long without sunscreen on, and _____, which you get from coming into contact with sharp objects.

PUZZLE
15·4

Crossword

Across

2. Short for influenza.
4. A bruise around your eye: A _____ eye.
6. Another word for pain.
7. _____ some medicine when you are sick.
8. Throw up.
9. _____ plenty of fluids when you are sick.
11. A cold symptom: A _____ nose.
12. An injury from touching a hot object.
13. Something you get during flu season: A flu _____.
15. A sign that you are sick.
17. Can't see clearly: Have blurred _____.
20. Not able to sleep.
23. A common hiker's injury: A _____ ankle.
26. Another word for sickness.
27. A long-lasting pain in the head.
28. A body's overreaction to something like pollen or cat hair.

Down

1. A time when you need a cast: A _____ bone.
2. A high body temperature.
3. _____ plenty of rest when you are sick.
5. A mild infection involving the nose and throat: The _____ cold.
10. A word used to describe physical harm to your body.
11. An area of red bumpy skin.
12. A swollen area under your skin (usually from being hit by something).
14. A pain caused by a cavity.
15. A cold symptom: A _____ throat.
16. Something you take to get better.
18. An injury from a bee.
19. A purple or blue mark under the skin as a result of an injury.
21. _____ a doctor when you are sick.
22. A desire to scratch something.
24. Get better.
25. Feel like you are going to fall or lose consciousness.

Word search: Common ailments *Find the following words in the grid.*

```
P O S H G C A H F B C O N S T I P A T I O N X I
T C C I B O S X E I B R O K E N B O N E I L A C
W G R C L M K K V T O S F B L I S T E R E V H H
O K A C U M J E E E X C O N G E S T I O N E P P
X F P U R O V K R N R H O G O C S S S Y H X U K
I S E P R N H C I W A Z G D R O B R S C R C N Q
N P T S E C M A B N S Y E C W U R L A N J X C Z
D R B T D O P E U Q H N S P M G N H A B E S X W
I A E O V L V A M H M Q H O Q H T N J C S H D U
G I I M I D Z L P V R R W C R O A O Y E K D H S
E N N A S I W B R U I S E Z O E D H N N W E E Z
S P S C I Z A L P B I O G T Y S T I N G O I Y U
T S O H O Z Q B U L G V E R G O H H A B G S F E
I Z M A N I M X S B P H U E R C W V R R T G E O
O E N C C N M N S A U J B Z T V J O E O R G E T
N F I H U E Y Z M N R S I E G A L A E A H I L
O L A E T S V O M I T I N G O J L K L T D T E C
D U W W J S E F F H P H E A D A C H E D T T L A
```

Allergies	Cough	Pain
Bite	Cut	Pus
Black eye	Diarrhea	Rash
Blister	Dizziness	Runny nose
Blurred vision	Fever	Scrape
Broken bone	Flu	Sore throat
Bruise	Headache	Sprain
Bump	Hiccups	Sting
Burn	Indigestion	Stomachache
Common cold	Injury	Toothache
Congestion	Insomnia	Vomiting
Constipation	Itchiness	

Idiom puzzle: Common ailments idioms and expressions *Complete the health-related idioms below. Use the shape symbols below the blanks to help you solve the missing blanks.*

1. Feeling ill: UNDER THE _ _ _ _ _ _
   27 ♥ 8 ♣ ♦ ♥ ▼

2. Feeling better: BACK ON ONE'S _ _ _ _ _
   ⊡ ♥ ♥ 17

3. Get some medicine: FILL A _ _ _ _ _ _ _ _ _ _ _ _ _
   ▲ ▼ ♥ ● ■ ▼ △ 5 ♣ △ 21 ♠

4. Not really sick: ALL IN YOUR _ _ _ _
   ♦ 7 ◐ ★

5. Have an operation: GO UNDER THE _ _ _ _ _ _
   12 ♠ △ ⊡ ♥

6. Very anxious about something: A BUNDLE OF _ _ _ _ _ _ _
   ♠ 19 ▼ ○ ♥ ●

7. A regular visit to the doctor: HAVE A _ _ _ _ _ _ _
   ■ ♦ 13 ■ Σ 15

8. Have a fever: RUN A _ _ _ _ _ _ _ _ _ _ _
   ♣ ♥ ♪ 4 ♥ ▼ 26 23 Σ ▼ ♥

9. A reason to take aspirins: A _ _ _ _ _ _ _ _ _ _ HEADACHE
   ● ▲ 6 △ ♣ ♣ △ ♠ ♦

10. Getting better: ON THE _ _ _ _ _
    ♪ ♥ ♠ 9

11. Getting better: ON THE _ _ _ _ TO RECOVERY
    ▼ 24 10 ★

12. Nothing wrong on a physical examination: A CLEAN BILL OF _ _ _ _ _ _ _
    ♦ 14 ◐ Ω ♣ 18

13. Very healthy: AS FIT AS A _ _ _ _ _ _ _
    ⊡ △ ★ ★ Ω ♥

14. Near death: ONE FOOT IN THE _ _ _ _ _ _
    ♦ ▼ 1 ○ ♥

15. An allergic reaction: _ _ _ FEVER
    ♦ ◐ 29

16. Doctor's orders: EAT A _ _ _ _ _ _ _ _ _ DIET
    28 Ω ◐ 2 22 ♥ ★

17. Doctor's orders: DRINK _ _ _ _ _ _ _ OF FLUIDS
    ▲ Ω ♥ ♠ ♣ 11

18. Doctor's orders: GET SOME _ _ _ _ _
    ▼ ♥ 16 ♣

19. Doctor's orders: GET _ _ _ _ _ _ _ _ EXERCISE
    ▼ ♥ ♦ Σ Ω 3 25

Code breaker: A proverb concerning health *Use the number code in puzzle 15·6 to solve the proverb.*

A balanced diet will help you stay healthy:

— — — — — — — — — — — — — — — — — — — — — — — — — — — —
1 2 3 4 5 6 7 8 9 10 11 12 13 14 15 16 17 18 19 20 21 22 23 24 25

— — — —
26 27 28 29

Government and citizenship

·16·

VOCABULARY

amendment
armed forces
bill
checks and balances
citizen
civil rights
community
Congress
Constitution
council

democracy
dictatorship
executive branch
federal/national
government service
governor
judicial branch
law
legislative branch

mayor
monarchy
municipal
president
representative
responsibilities
state/provincial
Supreme Court
tax

PUZZLE
16·1

Match-up *Match the words from the vocabulary box with these definitions.*

1. Branch of government that passes laws _____

2. Branch of government that enforces laws _____

3. Branch of government that oversees the court system used for resolving disputes _____

4. The level of government that governs the whole country _____

_____

5. The level of government below the federal government _____

_____

6. The level of government that governs a city _____

7. Head of the national government in the United States _____

8. Head of the state government in the United States _____

9. Head of the municipal government _____

10. A system of government where citizens vote to elect their leaders _____

_____

11. A system of government where the leader is a hereditary king or queen _____
_____

12. A system of government where one person has absolute power _____
_____

13. Basic freedoms and protections for citizens _____

14. Duties and obligations of citizens _____

15. The highest court in the United States _____

16. A written record of the basic principles that a government of a country must follow _____
_____

17. A change to a law or the constitution _____

18. A system that prevents any one group of people in government from obtaining too much
power _____

19. A proposed law that has yet to be voted on _____

20. A politician who represents you in government (who votes instead of you in government)
_____

Labeling: Citizens and governments *Attach the government-related labels to the
following lists of words.*

branches of government   government services   systems of government
citizen responsibilities   heads of government   taxes levied by governments

1. _____

income/sales/property

2. _____

executive/legislative/judicial

3. _____

police force/road building and maintenance/public schools

4. _____

president/governor/mayor

5. _____

pay taxes/obey the law/speak truthfully under oath

6. _____

democracy/monarchy/oligarchy/dictatorship

Fill in the blanks: Government and citizenship *Complete the following paragraphs by filling in the blanks using the words provided.*

Citizen rights and obligations

beliefs	express	obey	responsibilities	taxes
discriminated	member	race	rights	

A citizen is a _____ of a country or a community. Citizens of democratic

countries and communities have a balance of rights and responsibilities. _____

are basic freedoms and protections. For example, the law protects citizens from

being _____ against on grounds such as _____ or gender.

In these countries, citizens also have a right to follow their own religious _____

and _____ their opinions on political issues. Along with rights, citizens

have _____, which are their duties and obligations. For example, they have to

pay their _____ and _____ the law.

Government services

collect	firefighters	income	provide
emergency	good	maintained	services

One function of government is to provide _____ for its citizens. For example,

the government makes sure the roads are _____ and that rescue personnel

are available in times of _____. Many citizens in a country are paid by the

government to _____ services for the public _____. Teachers in

public schools, _____, and members of the armed forces are a few examples.

In order to fund these government services, the government has to _____ taxes

from its citizens. For example, governments often levy _____, sales, and

property taxes.

The legislative branch

bill	Congress	legislative	passes
branches	lawmakers	Parliament	vote

In many democratic countries, there are three main _____ of government.
The first branch is called the _____ branch, and its job is to pass new laws.
When _____ feel there is a need for a new law or a change to the legal
system, they introduce a _____. That bill is then debated on by the assembly
of lawmakers, called _____ in America and _____ in the
UK. Finally, a _____ is taken, and if enough lawmakers support the bill, it
_____ and becomes a law.

The executive and judicial branches

appeal	broken	executive	president	Supreme
armed	enforce	judicial	resolving	

The job of the _____ branch is to implement and _____ the
laws made by the legislative branch. The executive branch is also in charge of protecting the
country, and so it controls the _____ forces. In America, the _____
is the head of the executive branch. The _____ branch, on the other hand,
oversees the court system. Its job is to decide when laws are being _____. Part
of its function is _____ disputes within the legal system. When people are not
happy with court resolutions, they can _____ the decisions in higher courts. In
America, the _____ Court is the highest court in the nation, and its decisions
cannot be appealed.

Crossword

Across

1. A system of government where citizens vote to elect their leaders.

6. A place where legal disputes are resolved.

8. A document with the basic principles on which a country is governed.

9. The head of a municipal government.

11. The group of people that rule a country.

15. The highest court in the United States: The _____ Court.

Down

2. A system of government where the leader is a hereditary king or queen.

3. What government needs to prevent anyone from becoming too powerful: _____ and balances.

4. Choose your government.

5. Freedoms and protections that citizens are given.

6. A member of a country or a community with full rights.

7. A gathering of lawmakers.

Across (cont.)

17. The branch of government that runs the court system.

18. The branch of government that enacts laws that have been passed.

21. Money collected by the government.

22. Obligations and duties of citizens.

25. The head of the executive branch of government in the United States.

26. A rule that a government makes and citizens must obey.

Down (cont.)

10. A person who votes instead of you in the legislative assembly.

12. A system of government where one person (or a small group of people) has absolute power.

13. The branch of government that passes laws.

14. A time when people vote for their government.

16. Things the government provides for citizens:
Government _____.

19. Government at the level of the city.

20. Make sure people obey the law: _____ the law.

23. Citizens must _____ the law.

24. A proposed law that has not been voted on.

Word search: Government *Find the following words in the grid.*

```
A P E R E S P O N S I B I L I T I E S A P N D N
R R Z N Y Q E N V F I R E F I G H T E R S V R N
M O S D D T Q E A U M S S U P R E M E C O U R T
E V R S A O G V L T T A D E M O C R A C Y C C A
D I X T S D J I B H I J Y Z Y S L F E D E R A L
F N S Q U D C D G T S O C O N S T I T U T I O N
O C T J D N B I N S M O N A R C H Y C K D Q G W
R E E E U W R E E B I S N A H S A S S E M B L Y
C X A O I D D R V T G A R N L J C C I T I Z E N
E X C A Z I G O X L A N C A M E N D M E N T H R
S N H L S N U T A P E X E C U T I V E D I L N A
J B E E O N P I G O V E R N O R D B I L L F S E
R I R C H E C K S A N D B A L A N C E S V I R O
F P S V Q I L A W R E P R E S E N T A T I V E S
U E U T D N D M M M A O D I C T A T O R S H I P
W W M U N I C I P A L P R I M E M I N I S T E R
J X J R B S E R V I C E C O M M U N I T Y W F N
B P X Z R N T P C Y U H L E G I S L A T I V E C
```

Amendment	Executive	Police
Armed forces	Federal	President
Assembly	Firefighters	Prime minister
Bill	Governor	Province
Checks and balances	Judge	Representative
Citizen	Judicial	Responsibilities
Community	Law	Rights
Congress	Legislative	Service
Constitution	Mayor	State
Council	Monarchy	Supreme Court
Democracy	Municipal	Tax
Dictatorship	National	Teachers

Word paths: Government *Find and circle the secret words by following a connected path through the maze. Some words may overlap. Use the remaining letters to uncover a phrase related to government.*

T	U	T	C	H	T	S	E	R	V	I
I	■	I	■	G	■	H	■	E	■	C
T	N	O	R	I	M	A	Y	O	R	E
S	■	L	■	C	■	K	■	S	■	A
N	N	E	G	I	S	L	W	A	D	J
O	■	M	■	B	■	A	■	L	■	U
C	O	U	N	I	A	T	I	V	E	D
I	■	R	■	C	■	U	■	L	■	I
T	A	T	N	I	C	C	E	X	E	C
I	■	E	■	P	■	E	■	J	■	I
Z	E	N	L	A	S	G	D	U	L	A

1. A member of a country or a community. __ __ __ __ __ __ __

2. A place where legal disputes are resolved. __ __ __ __ __

3. The basic laws of a country that the government must follow. __ __ __ __ __ __ __ __ __ __ __ __

4. Basic freedoms and protections for citizens. __ __ __ __ __ __

5. A person who presides over a court. __ __ __ __ __

6. Government at the city level. __ __ __ __ __ __ __ __ __

7. The leader of a city. __ __ __ __ __

8. A rule that citizens must obey. __ __ __

9. Something the government provides for its citizens. __ __ __ __ __ __ __

10. Branch of government that passes laws. __ __ __ __ __ __ __ __ __ __ __

11. Branch of government that enforces laws. __ __ __ __ __ __ __ __ __ __

12. Branch of government that oversees the court system. __ __ __ __ __ __ __ __ __

What good government needs:

__ __ __ __ __ __   __ __ __   __ __ __ __ __ __ __ __

Geography

17

Maps and geography

VOCABULARY

Antarctic Circle
Arctic Circle
atlas
border
coast
compass rose
continent
contour lines
coordinates

equator
geography
globe
hemisphere
latitude
longitude
map key
ocean
physical map

political map
prime meridian
scale
terrain
the poles
topographical map
Tropic of Capricorn
Tropic of Cancer

PUZZLE 17·1

Word list: Things on a map *Match the vocabulary words with these definitions.*

1. A line on a map that goes from east to west _____

2. A line on a map that goes from north to south _____

3. Lines on a map that show elevations _____

4. A line on a map that divides countries _____

5. Zero degrees longitude _____

6. Zero degrees latitude _____

7. A line of latitude about 23 degrees north _____

8. A line of latitude about 23 degrees south _____

9. A line of latitude about 66 degrees north _____

10. A line of latitude about 66 degrees south _____

11. Something on a map that shows directions _____

12. Something that explains map symbols _____

13. Something that indicates how large things are _____

14. 90% latitude (north and south) _____

15. The physical features of land _____

16. A book of maps _____

17. A spherical map of the world _____

18. A map that shows countries and borders _____

19. A map that shows elevation using contour lines _____

20. A map that shows landforms like deserts, mountains, plains, and lakes _____

_____

_____

Labeling: Things on a map *Attach the climate-related labels to the following lists of words.*

lines of latitude   names of oceans   types of maps
names of continents   things used to decipher a map   ways to indicate elevation

1. _____   5. _____

Africa/Antarctica/South America   Arctic Circle
                                          Tropic of Cancer
2. _____

political/physical/topographical   6. _____

3. _____   colors
                                          contours
Atlantic/ Indian/Pacific

4. _____

compass rose/map key/scale

Matching: Geography collocations *Match the geographical words in the box with their collocations.*

Arctic   contour   prime   sea   topographical   Tropic

1. _____ map

2. _____ of Capricorn

3. _____ meridian

4. _____ Circle

5. _____ lines

6. _____ level

Fill in the blanks: Maps, continents, and oceans *Complete the following paragraphs by filling in the blanks using the words provided.*

Types of maps

borders   features   level   lines   physical   political   ranges   topographical

There are many different types of maps. Maps that show cities, countries, and the

_____ between countries are called _____ maps. Maps that

show land _____ such as mountain _____, deserts, plains, lakes,

and rivers are called _____ maps. Maps that show elevation in detail are called

_____ maps. These maps often use contour _____ or colors to

indicate elevation above sea _____.

Lines on a map

Circle   equator   location   Pole   south
coordination   latitude   longitude   prime

Maps use a variety of lines to indicate the _____ of things. Lines that run from

north to south are called lines of _____. Zero degrees longitude is called

the _____ meridian. Lines that go from east to west are called lines

of _____. Zero degrees latitude is called the _____. As you

go north from the equator, you pass through the _____ of Cancer and the

Arctic _____ until finally you reach the North _____ and

start heading _____ again. If you want to know exactly where something is

on Earth, you have to know its _____, which is a combination of latitude and

longitude.

Continents and oceans

Antarctica	combined	depends	oceans	south
Arctic	continents	Eurasia	Pacific	

_____ are the large landmasses that span the globe. The number of

continents there are _____ on where you went to school. Schools in some

countries of the world teach that there are seven continents, but others teach that there are

six or even five continents. For example, in some school systems, Europe and Asia are

_____ into a continent called _____. In other school

systems, North and _____ America are combined into a single continent

called America. A similar situation applies to the large saltwater bodies that cover the Earth

called _____. Traditionally, schools have taught that there are four oceans

called the Atlantic, the _____, the Arctic, and the Indian. However, some

scientists feel that the frigid _____ Ocean is too small to be called an

ocean and should be called a sea. Other scientists argue that the waters surrounding

_____ comprise another ocean called the Southern Ocean, which is distinct

from the Atlantic, Pacific, and Indian oceans.

Deciphering a map

capital	circle	compass	decipher	legend	reality	scale	symbols

Mapmakers usually include several tools that help you _____ a map. Often

they include a _____ rose to indicate the four directions: north, east, south,

and west. They also include a _____, which tells you how big things on the

map are in _____. As well, there is usually a _____ or a key

to help you understand the _____ used on the map. For examples, many

maps mark cities with a _____. _____ cities, however, are

often marked with a star inside a circle.

Crossword

Across

2. A map that shows you countries, cities, and borders.

5. The boundary between land and water.

6. A spherical map of the world.

8. A line of latitude: The _____ of Cancer

10. A large landmass such as Africa or Asia.

12. A city usually denoted by a star inside a circle: _____ city.

Down

1. A line on a map that indicates the same elevation.

3. Another word for position.

4. Lines on a map that go from north to south.

7. Zero degrees latitude.

9. Zero degrees longitude: The _____ meridian.

11. The height above sea level.

14. The study of the landforms, land features, and inhabitants of the Earth.

Across (cont.)

13. Another way to say map key.

15. A line of latitude: The Arctic _____ .

17. A map that shows you the elevation of the land using colors or contour lines.

19. A combination of latitude and longitude.

21. A book of maps.

22. Half of the globe.

24. Something on a map that explains what the symbols mean: Map _____ .

25. Lines on a map that go from east to west.

27. Something that tells you the directions on a map: The compass _____ .

Down (cont.)

16. How big something is on a map compared to its size in reality.

17. The land features of an area.

18. A large body of salt water such as the Pacific or Atlantic.

20. A line between countries.

23. Ninety degrees longitude: The North _____ .

26. A line where the day changes: The International _____ Line

Word search: Things on a map *Find the following words in the grid.*

```
D L K Q T N O R T H P O L E Y I P C D W C C Q U
M R U M Q R S P R I M E M E R I D I A N N E C H
G L O B E E O C S D S X E D L T Z C J R R S G R
T I G Q Q B Q P A S C O M P A S S R O S E U E J
O S Y B Z B D U I L D V U J P Y Q C W T I A C E
P C N N T V U W A C E S N N H H I L A W Y V L U
O O C M A P K E Y T O F O P L R Y N C N C C V U
G N I O V O K O Y C O F A V P O I S O R R W Q B
R T C T N M R R V S A R C A H D N I I I A G I S
A O T S Y T T Z A V G P C A R E T G C C U M O B
P U H U L N I L C O C F I O N A M C I K A Q G M
H R Z H U M T N E A O T O T V C I I T T S L R G
I L Q O C A M G E C A C W E A T E N S W U M H U
C I C A I M D O I N S P L E C L T R J P V D F P
A N W Q T P U P C E T E R R A I N P F Q H D E I
L E X Y Y B O R D E R L A T I T U D E E U E M M
G S I R M R I H B Z A V J C N Z N O P L K N R Z
P O L I T I C A L Q N N Y S O U T H P O L E Z E
```

Arctic Circle	Country	Ocean
Atlas	Elevation	Physical
Border	Equator	Political
Capital	Geography	Prime meridian
City	Globe	Scale
Coast	Hemisphere	South Pole
Compass rose	Latitude	Terrain
Continent	Longitude	Topographical
Contour lines	Map key	Tropic of Cancer
Coordinates	North Pole	Tropic of Capricorn

Geography and landforms

archipelago
atoll
canyon
cave
cavern
cliff
delta
estuary
glacier

hill
island
lake
landform
mountain range
peninsula
plain
plateau

reef
river basin
sand dune
slope
tributary
valley
volcano
waterfall

PUZZLE 17·7

Word list: Geographic landforms *Match the vocabulary words with these definitions.*

1. Land surrounded by water on three sides _____

2. Land completely surrounded by water _____

3. Water completely surrounded by land _____

4. A ring-shaped island formed from coral _____

5. A mountain created by magma forcing its way to the surface _____

6. A triangular landform at the mouth of a river _____

7. A shape or feature of land _____

8. A chain or group of islands _____

9. A chain or group of mountains _____

10. The side of a mountain _____

11. A steep slope _____

12. Flat lands _____

13. High flat land _____

14. A ridge of coral or rock submerged just below the water's surface _____

15. Thick ice that remains year-round _____

16. A place where the tide meets a river or stream _____

17. A river that joins a larger river _____

18. The land drained by a river and all its tributaries _____

Word sort: Geographic landforms *The following words are geographic landforms.*
Look up any words you don't know. Then sort the words into the following lists.

apex	coast	gulf	shore
bay	cove	inlet	straight
beach	creek	peak	stream
channel	fjord	river	summit

FLOWING BODIES OF FRESHWATER

_____

_____

NARROW BODIES OF WATER THAT SEPARATE
TWO LANDMASSES

_____

_____

BODIES OF WATER SURROUNDED BY LAND
ON THREE SIDES

_____

_____

SALTWATER BODIES THAT EXTEND DEEP
INTO THE LAND

_____

_____

THE TOP OF A MOUNTAIN

_____

_____

PLACES WHERE LAND MEETS THE WATER

_____

_____

_____

Fill in the blanks: Geography and landforms *Complete the following paragraphs*
by filling in the blanks using the words provided.

River basins

basin	delta	estuary	flows	mouth	sedimentation	tide	tributary

A river is a body of fresh water that _____ over land to a lake, sea, or ocean.

Sometimes one river is joined by another river called a _____. The region that

is drained by a river and all of its tributaries is called a river _____. Where a

river meets a larger body of water, a triangular-shaped landform called a _____

often forms through the process of _____. The delta sits at the _____

of the river. If the river flows into a sea or an ocean, an _____ can also form, which is a place where the tide and the river meet. At high _____, the salt water from the ocean can flow back into the river mouth.

Highlands

cliff   crust   formed   peak   plateau   ranges   similar   slope   summit

Mountains are _____ by the slow but powerful movements of the Earth's _____. When one plate pushes against another, the crust folds up and creates mountain _____. The top of a mountain is called the _____ or _____. The side of the mountain is called a _____. If the slope is very steep, then it is called a _____. Hills are _____ to mountains, but they are not as high or as steep. A _____ is another type of highland, but, unlike mountains and hills, it is relatively flat on top.

Where land meets sea

archipelago   atolls   bay   eruptions   gulf   peninsula   shore   surrounded

Many different landforms are created along the land-sea boundary called the _____. For example, land that juts out into the ocean and is surrounded by water on three sides is called a _____. However, when the water is surrounded by land on three sides it is called a _____ or a _____. Land that is completely _____ by water is called an island. An _____ is a chain or group of islands. Some islands are formed through volcanic _____. Other ring-shaped islands called _____ are built from coral reefs.

Land sculpted by ice

age   boulders   connected   eroded   fjords   glaciers   level   temperature

An ice _____ is a period when the Earth's surface _____ is significantly cooler. During ice ages, large masses of slowly moving ice called _____ formed in many parts of the world. As these glaciers flowed, they _____ the land around them, forming valleys and canyons. In Scandinavia, giant _____ were carved out so that now the ocean extends great distances inland. As well, huge _____ that now seem out of place were in fact carried great distances by moving ice sheets to where they rest today. During these glacial periods, there was so much ice on land that the sea _____ actually dropped and places that are separated by water today were _____ by land bridges.

Crossword

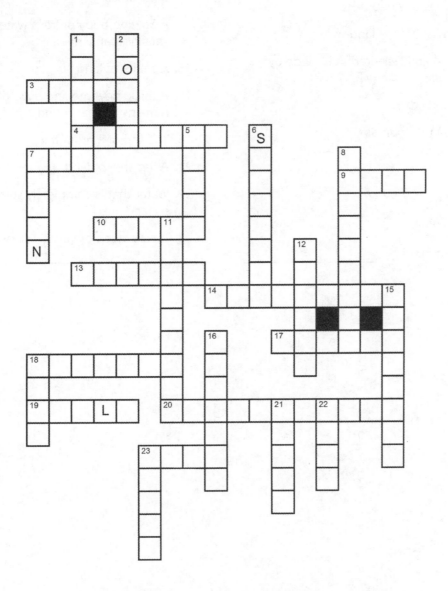

Across

3. A triangle-shaped land at the mouth of a river.

4. Place where a river and tidal waters meet.

7. Water that is surrounded by land on three sides.

9. Submerged ridge of coral or rock just below the surface of the water.

10. The side of a mountain.

13. Land that is completely surrounded by water.

Down

1. Land between two mountains.

2. Where the land meets the sea.

5. A chain of mountains: A mountain _____.

6. A narrow body of water that divides two landmasses.

7. The land that a river and its tributaries drain:
River _____.

8. A river that joins a larger river.

Across (cont.)

14. Water that flows over a cliff.

17. A valley with steep sides.

18. A high flat area of land.

19. A ring-shaped island that is made by coral reefs.

20. An island chain.

23. A hole in a mountain.

Across (cont.)

11. Land that is surrounded by water on three sides.

12. A flowing body of fresh water that is smaller than a river.

15. A shape of land.

16. A thick, slow moving mass of ice that remains all year-round.

18. The top of a mountain.

21. A flat area of land.

22. Water that is completely surrounded by land.

23. A very steep or vertical slope.

Word search: Geography and landforms *Find the following words in the grid.*

```
W B E B P Q E S T U A R Y E C A N Y O N K C F E
P N U W J F I S L A N D H D G S A N D D U N E K
L M N A K H X N D B Q M D I U B F D G O C E T P
A A Z T H C U Y C E R X E H L T F U E P G X N P
T R V E B D R T Q F P X L B F L R L N N S J G K
E C O R L U P E S L E E T J Y I M I A M L M V C
A H L F J O R D E P E O A E F A S R B G H H I I
U I C A V E R N A K F V L K E A N S C U R G O N
J P A L P O X S A Z E L R R B I V T H C T V T M
P E N L P V O L N S A S T R A I G H T O E A Z L
G L O U F G F L L V T S E T S G E G W U R S R K
B A M G N V E V Q H H V N K E N U L Y G T E M Y
E G C F S N C G V W I U Z X O S O L S E B K L T
A O Y O N U S X R R O P L A I N V I U F J P C V
C I M A A F M L G M L A N D F O R M N R E E I A
H O H F E S H M O C L I F F Z Y A T O L L D U L
W C V E J L T D I P E N I N S U L A Y D E I R W
M K R E H C M W U T E G G L A C I E R G B T S A
```

Apex	Estuary	Plateau
Archipelago	Fjord	Reef
Atoll	Glacier	River basin
Bay	Gulf	Sand dune
Beach	Hill	Shore
Canyon	Inlet	Slope
Cavern	Island	Straight
Channel	Lake	Stream
Cliff	Landform	Summit
Coast	Mountain range	Tributary
Cove	Peak	Valley
Creek	Peninsula	Volcano
Delta	Plain	Waterfall

Word paths: Landforms *Find and circle the secret words by following a connected path through the maze. Some words may overlap. Use the remaining letters to uncover an idiom related to landforms.*

S	U	L	T	U	T	A	H	I	E	R
N	■	A	■	B	■	R	■	C	■	N
I	E	T	R	I	T	Y	N	A	I	I
N	■	P	P	■	O	■	L	■	A	
E	D	E	O	L	F	N	T	G	P	L
P	■	L	A	■	H	■	E	■	V	
G	O	T	A	T	E	A	U	L	L	A
A	■	I	C	■	C	■	E	■	I	
L	E	P	E	L	I	F	F	Y	B	S
A	■	I	E	■	E	■	R	■	L	
R	C	H	S	L	O	P	G	D	N	A

1. A chain of islands. __ __ __ __ __ __ __ __ __ __

2. Land that juts out into the water. __ __ __ __ __ __ __ __ __

3. A river that joins a larger river. __ __ __ __ __ __ __ __ __

4. Land between mountains. __ __ __ __ __ __

5. A slowly flowing mass of ice. __ __ __ __ __ __ __ __

6. Triangle-shaped land at the mouth of a river. __ __ __ __ __

7. The side of a mountain. __ __ __ __ __

8. A vertical slope on a mountain. __ __ __ __ __ __

9. A valley with steep sides. __ __ __ __ __ __

10. Land completely surrounded by water __ __ __ __ __ __

11. A relatively flat region. __ __ __ __ __

12. Flat land at a high elevation. __ __ __ __ __ __ __

A small part of a larger problem:

__ __ __   __ __ __   __ __   __ __ __   __ __ __ __ __ __

Word scramble: Archipelago *Find the words within the word "archipelago." You can use the letters in any order, but you can only use each letter once. Hint: Use the code breaker to the right to help you solve the words.*

ARCHIPELAGO

CLUES	ANSWERS	CODE BREAKER
1. A sound that bounces back	_ _ _ _	x 1 2 3
2. A job around the house	_ _ _ _ _	4 5 x 6 x
3. Another word for copy	_ _ _ _ _ _ _	7 x 8 9 x x 10
4. The opposite of boy	_ _ _ _	11 x 12 13
5. A month of the year	_ _ _ _ _	x 14 15 x 16
6. A thick sheet of ice that slowly flows	_ _ _ _ _ _ _	17 18 x 19 x x 20
7. Something superheroes wear	_ _ _ _	4 22 21 x
8. A fossil fuel	_ _ _ _	23 24 10 16
9. Another word for equipment	_ _ _ _	17 25 x 12
10. A type of fruit	_ _ _ _ _	26 x x 1 27
11. A group of singers	_ _ _ _ _	19 5 24 x x
12. Another word for jump	_ _ _ _	18 28 x 21
13. An oyster's treasure	_ _ _ _ _	14 x x 6 13
14. A person who fibs	_ _ _ _	18 x 22 7
15. A song at Christmas	_ _ _ _ _	1 x 20 x 9
16. A prediction of the future	_ _ _ _ _ _ _	24 6 x 4 13 x
17. Another word for danger	_ _ _ _ _	14 25 6 x 9
18. A type of crop	_ _ _ _	20 x 4 28
19. Something you comb	_ _ _ _	2 x x 7
20. A person who does great deeds	_ _ _ _	2 25 15 29
21. The opposite of expensive	_ _ _ _ _	4 27 x x 8
22. Something you use to row a boat	_ _ _	29 22 12
23. The center of an apple	_ _ _ _	23 3 6 x
24. A strong windstorm	_ _ _ _	11 x 16 25
25. A bird or cricket sound	_ _ _ _	19 5 x x 8
26. A speed competition	_ _ _ _	15 22 4 x
27. Hunt an animal illegally	_ _ _ _ _	26 3 x 23 x
28. Something ships or planes transport	_ _ _ _ _	23 10 x 11 29

Disasters

VOCABULARY

avalanche	earthquake	mine explosion	tornado
blizzard	epidemic	nuclear meltdown	toxic contamination
building fire	famine	oil spill	train derailment
civil war	flood	plane crash	tsunami
collapsed bridge	gas leak	power outage	typhoon
collapsed building	heat wave	riot	volcanic eruption
cyclone	hurricane	shipwreck	war
drought	landslide	terrorist attack	wildfire

PUZZLE
18·1

Matching: Disasters *Match these descriptions with the previous vocabulary words.*

1. A disease that has spread widely _____

2. A time when the ground shakes _____

3. Crops dying from lack of rain _____

4. A time when electricity is cut _____

5. Conflict within a country _____

6. Widespread starvation _____

7. Lava coming out of a mountain _____

8. A large mass of snow sliding down a mountain _____

9. Conflict among countries _____

10. Rivers overflowing from rain _____

11. A period of high temperatures _____

12. A large devastating ocean wave _____

13. A forest or brush fire _____

14. A severe snowstorm _____

15. A mob of angry citizens _____

16. Rocks and mud sliding down a mountain _____

Word sort: Natural versus human-caused disasters *Choose six disasters from the box that could be classified as natural disasters and six that could be classified as human-caused disasters.*

NATURAL DISASTERS   HUMAN-CAUSED DISASTERS

_____   _____

_____   _____

_____   _____

_____   _____

Identification: Disasters *Read the following sentences and decide what disaster has occurred.*

1. A radiation leak is forcing people to evacuate. _____

2. People are throwing sandbags along the river banks to protect property. _____

_____

3. Lava is creeping down the mountain. _____

4. Rescuers are frantically trying to dig people out of the snow. _____

_____

5. The coast guard is searching for survivors among the floating debris. _____

_____

6. People are lighting candles so they can see in the dark. _____

7. Doctors are frantically searching for a cure and hospitals are overcrowded. _____

_____

8. Sea birds are washing up on shore and people are cleaning the beaches. _____

_____

Crossword

Across

1. A time when too much rain causes rivers to overflow.

5. A person who lives through a disaster.

6. People who rescue others at sea.

8. A serious and dangerous situation that requires immediate action.

12. A ship that has sunk.

14. An angry mob that vandalizes a city.

15. A mass of snow or ice that slides down a mountain.

21. A twisting column of air.

Down

1. A time when many people are starving.

2. A time when the electricity is not working: A power _____.

3. A time when lack of rain causes crops to wither.

4. Another word for forest fire.

7. A large deadly wave on the ocean.

9. A time when lava and ash come out of a volcano.

10. A severe winter snowstorm.

11. A dangerous out-of-control situation at nuclear power plants: A nuclear _____.

Across (cont.)

22. A conflict between nations.

23. A war between groups within a country: _____ war.

25. Hazardous chemicals leaking into the soil: Toxic _____.

26. A prolonged period of really hot weather: A heat _____.

Down (cont.)

13. A serious accident: A plane _____.

16. A vehicle that carries injured or sick people.

17. A time when the ground shakes.

18. A large tropical storm in the Atlantic Ocean.

19. A mass of rocks and earth that slide down a mountain.

20. A place where sick and injured people are treated.

23. Global warming: Climate _____.

24. A time when oil is floating on the ocean: An oil _____.

PUZZLE 18·5

Fill in the blanks: Natural disasters *Complete the following paragraphs by filling in the blanks using the words provided.*

Drought

consequences   crops   erosion   famine   livestock   migrate   precipitation

A drought is a time when a region receives too little _____ for an extended period. Droughts can have serious _____ for the people and environment where they occur: Natural vegetation and farmers' _____ wither without water, which reduces the ability of the land to support both wildlife and _____. As food resources decrease, malnutrition and _____ become widespread. This forces many people to _____ to other regions in search of food and a means of living. As well, the lack of vegetation covering the ground leads to _____ of soil and huge dust storms.

Flood

bridges   flood   life   river   submerged
damage   heavy   rescuers   sandbags

The opposite of a drought is a _____, which can occur when _____ rains fall on a region. As water spills over river banks, people try to control floods using _____, but often they are overwhelmed by the forces of nature. Flooding is especially dangerous to communities on lowlands in _____ basins. Floods can cause loss of _____ and property _____. To make matters worse, it is hard for _____ to reach flood victims because roads are _____ under water and _____ are washed out, leaving many people stranded.

Hurricanes

cyclones   evacuate   ocean   property   rains   typhoons   windows   winds

When a large tropical storm develops over the _____, the government warns citizens to _____ the coast because a hurricane is coming. Hurricanes bring strong _____ and heavy _____. The winds shatter _____ and cause roofs to blow off of buildings. To make matters worse, the rains can cause severe flooding, adding to the already extensive _____ damage. In other parts of the world, hurricanes are called _____ or _____.

Volcanoes

ash   catastrophic   eruptions   lava   molten   toxic

Volcanic _____ are another deadly natural disaster. When _____ rock called magma pushes its way to the surface of the earth, it can cause a _____ explosion: _____ pours down the mountainside burning anything in its path. _____ is thrown into the atmosphere causing sunsets to glow red for months. Volcanoes also release _____ gases that can quickly kill animals and people for miles around.

Earthquakes

casualties   collapse   epidemic   lack   lethal   pipes   rubble   sewer

Earthquakes are among the most _____ of natural disasters. When the ground shakes, buildings _____ and people become trapped under the _____. Fires break out and because water _____ are broken during the earthquake, the fires are difficult to control. In fact, sometimes the fires cause more _____ than the earthquakes themselves. To make matters worse, the _____ of clean drinking water and the broken _____ pipes can allow disease to spread causing an _____.

Matching: Disasters *The words listed here are used to describe disasters. Look up any words you don't know.*

a casualty	a victim	dig through rubble	search for survivors
a catastrophe	calamity	donate to charity	survivors
a disaster	clean up	evacuate people	the coast guard
a firefighter	clear roads	rebuild	the National Guard
an accident	contact loved ones	refugees	treat the injured
an aid worker	crash	remove debris	volunteer to help
a rescue worker	deliver aid	rescue survivors	wreck

Match the words with the following descriptions. If more than one answer is possible, choose any one of the possible answers to fill the blank.

1. Give money or goods to help _____

2. People who flee disaster areas _____

3. A person who delivers aid _____

4. Get rid of fallen trees on roads _____

5. Move people out of a danger area _____

6. A person who saves lives _____

7. People who live through disasters _____

8. Provide medical assistance _____

9. Make something again _____

10. Move the bricks and concrete of a collapsed building _____

Word sort: Disaster vocabulary *Sort the words in puzzle 18·6 into the following categories.*

PEOPLE INVOLVED IN DISASTERS	THINGS PEOPLE DO TO HELP	EMERGENCY SITUATIONS
_____	_____	_____
_____	_____	_____
_____	_____	_____
_____	_____	_____

Identification: Who are they talking about *Read the following sentences and decide which of the people involved in disasters are being talked about.*

1. They are searching the ocean for survivors of the shipwreck. _____

_____

2. They had to flee their homes when the war approached. _____

_____

3. After the earthquake, he was injured but he could still walk. _____

_____

4. She is delivering blankets and food to people who lost their homes. _____

_____

5. She is using a hose to put out the blaze. _____

Matching: Disaster collocations *Match the words listed here with their collocations.*

collapsed	heat	nuclear	sole
death	loss	property	toxic
first	natural	severe	volcanic

1. _____ survivor

2. _____ disaster

3. _____ eruption

4. _____ weather

5. _____ building

6. _____ wave

7. _____ responder

8. _____ contamination

9. _____ of life

10. _____ meltdown

11. _____ toll

12. _____ damage

Word search: Disasters *Find the following words in the grid.*

```
V O L C A N I C E R U P T I O N R V K Z D N C N
L N P L C Q F N N L C X L M B A B R H O P D W V
A R I I U Q M M E T X L F A W P T A O C M O Y N
N R I R M I H U R R I C A N E L D L J X D W U L
D W R O E A D R S P G E B U E A F C U T C A C T
S V H E Q S I B S I N T K L H N V E L L E C N E
L R R O F M C L J O Y E B Y D E H E O N K E G V
I P W S A U I U L W L B T Y O C M U N R M D B A
D K B N N O G C E V U L N C N R S O F L I G U C
E O U D R P Y E B R A S P A A A I Z I R E E K U
E S I Y I C V C E U W L L E C S Z A B T A P F A
T Z L T Q I X C S X O A L J O H R E S X E I L T
T M D C O E P A F F V C M L Z E S A T V T D Z E
R D I D V R C F U A U A P F D P W H A Z B E P W
T U N M X F N M D N Y X O N A C G W A P J M F C
G M G N W N I A C B E N I L I U T R I O T I O U
Q S F A M I N E D E O A L X O A J Q U V D C R D
L C I K R X Q Y N O R O O R E R T M I R M L E H
O O R A O T V I H T C T D H U P I A A I G U S N
B I E G V E M P J H R A B N B T S Z V E X K T J
S Q N A H A Y R A A K N Y G C P Z J J Q Z K F O
K T T I A T G A S L E A K I S I Z X P X M Y I K
E A R T H Q U A K E U D V M L V Q B G D K U R K
R A D I A T I O N L E A K B J O I A P V L X E H
```

Avalanche	Forest fire	Rescue
Blizzard	Gas leak	Riot
Building fire	Heat wave	Rubble
Casualty	Hurricane	Tornado
Cyclone	Landslide	Toxic waste
Drought	Mine explosion	Train derailment
Earthquake	Nuclear meltdown	Tsunami
Epidemic	Oil spill	Typhoon
Evacuate	Plane crash	Victim
Famine	Radiation leak	Volcanic eruption
Flood	Refugee	War

PUZZLE 18·11

Word scramble: Volcanic eruption *Find the words described within the phrase "volcanic eruption." You can use the letters in any order, but you can only use each letter once.*

VOLCANIC ERUPTION

HINT: USE THE CODE BREAKER TO THE RIGHT TO HELP YOU SOLVE THE WORDS.

CLUES	ANSWERS	CODE BREAKER
1. A place to swim	_ _ _ _ _	1 x x 2
2. A thing to catch mice	_ _ _ _ _	3 x x 4
3. A hard metal	_ _ _ _ _	5 6 x x
4. The seed of an oak tree	_ _ _ _ _ _	x 7 8 x x
5. A copy of a person	_ _ _ _ _ _	33 9 x 10 x
6. Transportation on rails	_ _ _ _ _ _	11 x 12 x x
7. A vegetable that makes you cry	_ _ _ _ _	13 x x x 14
8. The region around the North Pole	_ _ _ _ _ _	15 6 16 x x 32
9. A type of fuel	_ _ _ _	18 8 x 17
10. Another word for prisoner	_ _ _ _ _ _ _ _	18 x 34 x x 31 x
11. A road through a mountain	_ _ _ _ _ _	20 21 x x x x
12. An ideal place	_ _ _ _ _ _	21 x x 1 5 15
13. Something that gives a discount	_ _ _ _ _ _ _	18 22 x 4 x 23
14. The middle of the day	_ _ _ _ _	23 24 x x
15. A creature from outer space	_ _ _ _ _ _	25 17 x x x
16. Very old	_ _ _ _ _ _ _ _	12 x 33 x x x 3
17. A piece of metal money	_ _ _ _ _	16 22 x x
18. Another word for persuade	_ _ _ _ _ _ _ _ _	32 13 x 31 x x 26 x
19. A crazy person	_ _ _ _ _ _ _	2 21 29 x 11 x 16
20. The opposite of rude	_ _ _ _ _ _ _	x x 9 x 27 x
21. A winter wonder that hangs from your roof	_ _ _ _ _ _	28 7 x 7 x x
22. Wet weather	_ _ _ _ _	30 x x 29
23. A criminal at sea	_ _ _ _ _ _	34 5 x x 27 x
24. A person who judges movies	_ _ _ _ _ _	18 x x 20 x 18
25. A large body of salt water	_ _ _ _ _ _	8 26 x x 10
26. Another word for agree	_ _ _ _ _ _	33 x 14 33 21 30
27. A mythical half-human creature	_ _ _ _ _ _ _	32 x 23 3 25 x 30
28. Another word for place	_ _ _ _ _ _ _ _	2 8 33 x x 28 24 x

Answer key

1   Movies

1·1   1. script   2. dialogue   3. fantasy   4. family   5. science fiction   6. plot
7. crime   8. comedy   9. special effects   10. historical drama   11. documentary
12. scenes   13. climax   14. setting   15. horror   16. costumes   17. mystery
18. animation

1·2   1. action, adventure, animation, comedy, crime, documentary, family, fantasy, historical
drama, horror, mystery, road movie, romance, romantic comedy, science fiction, thriller
2. acting, character, cinematography, climax, costumes, dialogue, mood, plot, scenes,
script, setting, special effects

1·3   1. thumbs-up   2. thumbs-down   3. thumbs-up   4. thumbs-up   5. mixed
6. thumbs-up   7. thumbs-up   8. thumbs-down

1·4   **People in movies:** actors, role, starring, voices, supporting, cameo, extras, stunt

       Characters: characters, dialogue, costume, protagonist, main, antihero, antagonist, villain

       Setting and scenes: time, place, set, take, future, mood, horror, scene

       Plot: plot, synopsis, formulaic, car, sequence, twist

       Critics: reviews, rave, thumbs-up, pan, thumbs-down, mixed

1·5   1. sequel   2. scene   3. twist   4. antihero   5. costume   6. trilogy   7. script
8. dialogue   9. cast   10. romance   11. synopsis   12. role   13. stunt   14. rave
15. setting

       Hidden message: Movie phrase: a box office success

1·6   1. *Avatar*   2. *Les Miserables*   3. *The Lord of the Rings*   4. *Toy Story*   5. *Life of Pi*
6. *Titanic*   7. *Men in Black*   8. *Jurassic Park*   9. *The Sixth Sense*

1·7   1. cast   2. role   3. B movie   4. trailer   5. film crew   6. critic   7. synopsis
8. blockbuster

1·8   1. screen adaptation   2. computer graphics   3. movie buff   4. rave review
5. plot twist   6. cameo appearance   7. car chase   8. stunt performer
9. road movie   10. special effects   11. lead role   12. science fiction

1·9   1. Words seen on a movie screen   2. People who make movies   3. Scenes from an
action movie   4. People who watch movies   5. Equipment needed to make
movies   6. Words used to describe movie quality   7. Things heard in a
movie   8. Words used to describe an actor's role   9. Equipment needed to show movies

Horizontal (*Across*)

2. Special 6. Panned 8. Theater 9. Film 10. Plot 11. Blockbuster 15. Setting
16. Track 17. Science 19. Place 22. Subtitles 23. Action 24. Star 25. Documentary
26. Character 29. Critic 31. Genre 32. Crew 33. Rave 34. Fantasy

Vertical (*Down*)

1. Sequel 3. Play 4. Credits 5. Climax 7. Actor 9. Formulaic 12. Cast 13. Scenes
14. Synopsis 15. Script 18. Costume 20. Animation 21. Cameo 25. Dialogue 27. Horror
28. Role 29. Cinema 30. Comedy

```
F Z S S A N T A G O N I S T V T I Q M Q L N
A T M C B S C E N E P R O T A G O N I S T G
N D I R E C T O R S O U N D T R A C K W R O
T U L I S S O S P E C I A L E F F E C T S U
A Z S P A G S S F X H G T N O T V N S K R U
S C R T H E A T E R D O E P K O F P E V I
Y E U P A Z U V L U M M M L Y I U S T U N T
I L D Y W R Y G T Z M A E K T O C C E K B S
L E U O R E V I E W C E Y C R V A U B A R O
H B L O C K B U S T E R A I F R G C B O V A
B R P P C U C O M E D Y X T A O O B T J Z A
C I U W R P M Y W Y T G C H L W U C Y O J N
C T H R I L L E R M S T C A D V E N T U R E
I Y C B T A X O N T I T I B C J F V A G D S
N V T J I W C A T T H D E N O M T I X N Q U
E Z E Y C L I M A X A Z M R G O P F L O J W
M Z Q R O M A N C E R R P O Y W U B O M V U
A F J A N I M A T I O N Y R O O F A M I L Y
```

1. blue 2. bust 3. closet 4. lock 5. lobster 6. crust 7. cub 8. tusk 9. luck 10. truck
11. rocket 12. sub 13. broke 14. lose 15. ours 16. belt 17. cube 18. cure 19. score
20. role 21. close 22. trouble 23. rob 24. scrub 25. struck

2 Television and entertainment

1. Celebrity/star (possibly host) 2. Agent 3. Viewer 4. Commercials 5. Infomercial 6. Fan
7. Gossip 8. Talk show 9. Game show 10. Sitcom 11. Soap opera 12. Makeover 13. Cartoon
14. Newscast 15. Prime time 16. Paparazzi 17. Host 18. Episode 19. Privacy 20. Rerun

1. shows that have hosts 2. famous people 3. public renown 4. programming that advertises
5. people who watch shows 6. shows with multiple episodes

Prime time TV: prime, evening, networks, advertising, consequence, popular, viewers, rush, drive

Television programming: shows, sitcoms, apartment, talk, host, game, contestants, reality, newscasts

Advertising: public, advertising, commercials, volume, bathroom, placement, background, infomercials, benefits

The paparazzi: fans, fascinated, camera, relationship, crime, scandal, paparazzi, photo, privacy

Horizontal (*Across*)

1. Paparazzi 3. Game show 5. Privacy 6. Sitcom 8. Public 12. Fan 13. Newscast
15. Eye 17. Rerun 18. Perform 19. Placement 21. Audience 24. Reality show 25. Guest
26. Series 27. Studio 28. Cartoon

Vertical (*Down*)

2. Ratings 3. Gossip 4. Talk show 7. Makeover 9. Contestant 10. Commercial
11. Viewer 12. Fame 14. Soap opera 16. Prime time 20. Celebrity 22. Episode 23. Host

2·5

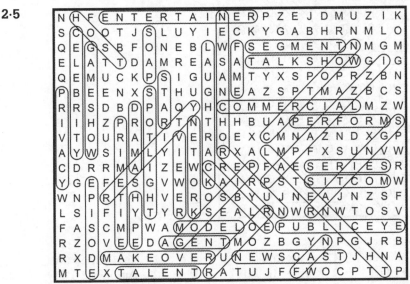

2·6

1. episode 2. contestant 3. model 4. talk show 5. cartoon 6. prime time
7. commercial 8. reality 9. perform 10. fan 11. celebrity 12. sitcom 13. act

Hidden message: Your claim to fame

3 Food and cooking

3·1

1. mix/stir 2. marinate 3. grease 4. pare/peel 5. deep fry 6. cube/dice 7. bake 8. boil
9. simmer 10. preheat 11. drain/strain 12. pour 13. roast 14. steam 15. fry 16. grill
17. smoke

3·2

1. cooking appliances 2. cooking apparel 3. spices 4. condiments 5. fruits and vegetables
6. cooking utensils 7. types of meat 8. shellfish 9. dairy products

3·3

1. a clove 2. a bowl 3. a loaf 4. a cup 5. a bottle 6. a head 7. a dash 8. a jar

3·4

Cooking utensils: utensils, pot, pan, flip, spatula, ladle, strainer, measuring, recipes

Food preparation: meal, ingredients, shopping, counter, chop, cutting, handling, mitts

Making bread: mix, flour, knead, cover, rise, loaf, preheat, bake

Making pizza: grease, rolling, spread, grate, sprinkle, toppings, pepperoni, oven, crust

Making chili: meat, drain, diced, simmer, stirring, ladle, serve, shredded

```
M E A S U R I N G C U P X U Y D S E A F O O D C
V W R D T N I Z D F G I A Q A V Z C M K Y J Q R
E K X I D O E H F P M R K L A W W V T R C K W O
Q Q K Q U F V P S E A V E U Y Z S I K O C K Z
J H D D A I S E R O A S T T F M A P O D N M P
G S P Y U R C H O P N U T W E T D A B A I Q G I
W A P O U L T R Y K B C F A Y B L K R A T R Z B
W A B I N G R E D I E N T S P Q O E R I C U I R
W P K Y C Q P O T S Y F P T A Q K T Z X N Z L D
N R D N S E Y A E I E Y O I C A S O Q K Z A M A
U O J J H R E L L Q I R R B Z Q S L I C E T B
T N O R F Y B I D K W X K A R M I C R O W A V E
E H I T I A Q A J O V E N S I M M E R C M M N Z
N H J K T B L H N G R I L L U U D A M M B H V Y
S A G E P X U A H F P I D G P U F W C R D J Y V
I M G T P E P T L U K E I B E E F U E N G A C B
L E J T O R L I S O V G C F E L B H I G M E C G
V A O L V Q X X W T I E B L R E C I P E T N L
```

3·6

Horizontal (*Across*)

2. Peel   3. Boil   4. Stove   6. Beef   7. Cup   9. Kettle   10. Recipe   11. Pan   12. Spatula
13. Roast   14. Microwave   18. Oven   19. Mitts   21. Mix   22. Dice   23. Apron   24. Fry
25. Dairy   26. Bowl   28. Simmer   29. Ingredients

Vertical (*Down*)

1. Kitchen   2. Pot   4. Spice   5. Vegetable   6. Bake   8. Pork   11. Poultry   12. Strain
15. Counter   16. Board   17. Shellfish   19. Measuring   20. Condiment   21. Marinate   27. Ladle

3·7   1. grill   2. recipe   3. dice   4. stir   5. simmer   6. slice   7. spatula   8. dairy   9. ingredient
10. roast   11. counter   12. microwave   13. marinate   14. bake

3·8   1. cream   2. food   3. icing   4. peas   5. carrot   6. apple   7. milk   8. bacon   9. pancake
10. pie   11. nut   12. mustard   13. pickle   14. potato   15. gravy   16. cheese   17. salt
18. candy   19. fruit

Code breaker: a proverb related to food: If life gives you lemons, make lemonade.

4   City life and country life

4·1   1. bank   2. library   3. gas station   4. crosswalk   5. gallery/museum   6. restaurant   7. museum
8. apartment   9. sidewalk   10. post office   11. airport   12. pharmacy   13. stadium
14. intersection   15. alley   16. hospital   17. warehouse   18. parking lot

4·2   1. housing   2. public transportation   3. cultural facilities   4. medical facilities   5. transport
infrastructure   6. entertainment venues   7. areas of a city   8. educational facilities   9. retail vendors

4·3

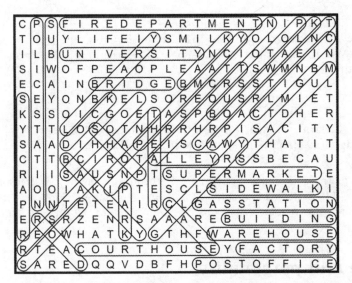

4·4   Quotation 1: City life is millions of people being lonesome together.

Quotation 2: This city is what it is because its citizens are what they are.

4·5   ## Horizontal (*Across*)

1. Home   2. Museum   4. School   6. Prison   8. Subway   10. Suburb   11. Crowd
13. Gallery   15. Mayor   17. Factory   18. Gym   19. Bank   20. Stop   21. Court   25. Department
27. Crime   28. Apartment   31. Lot   32. Rush   33. Road   34. Alley

Vertical (*Down*)

1. Hospital   3. Skyscraper   4. Station   5. Library   7. Intersection   9. Sidewalk
10. Smog   12. Playground   14. Urban   16. Restaurant   21. Café   22. Theater   23. Hotel
24. Airport   26. Park   29. Post   30. Mall

4·6   **Facilities:** advantage, medical, clinics, college, library, park, public

Culture and entertainment: theater, restaurant, stadium, gallery, history, nightlife, dancing, friends

City traffic: congestion, commuting, rush, bumper, standstill, honking, park

Pollution: problem, smog, noise, running, waste, drink

City infrastructure: infrastructure, bridges, water, sewer, crime, department, emergency, taxes

4·7   1. public   2. subway   3. pollution   4. station   5. traffic   6. sewer   7. office   8. crime
9. department

4·8   1. Feast or famine   2. Bumper to bumper   3. Tit for tat

4·9   1. livestock   2. cattle   3. woodlands   4. skyscrapers   5. resource industries   6. agriculture
7. smog   8. wildlife

4·10   **Work in the country:** rural, agriculture, crops, livestock, farmers, ranchers, resource, forestry

Country life: hustle, fields, wildlife, fresh, starry, traffic, crime

Exodus from the country: natural, opportunities, education, university, drawn, venues, nightlife, cost

4·11   1. cattle   2. sheep   3. horses   4. corn   5. rice   6. wheat   7. crops   8. field   9. tractor
10. trees   11. axes   12. saws   13. ore   14. mine

Horizontal (*Across*)

2. Harvest   5. Autumn   6. Ore   7. Rancher   10. Fish   12. Saw   15. Crow
16. Scarecrow   18. Spring   20. Wheat   21. Rural   22. Starry   25. Agriculture   28. Fresh
30. Crops   31. Farmer   32. Retire.

Vertical (*Down*)

1. Miner   2. Horse   3. Seeds   4. Barn   5. Axe   8. Corn   9. Resource   11. Livestock
13. Logger   14. Plow   17. Cottage   19. Irrigation   20. Wildlife   23. Rice   24. Tractor
26. Rooster   27. Cattle   29. Hike.

4·13   1. hero   2. north   3. east   4. mother   5. moose   6. rose   7. throne   8. stone   9. treason
10. math   11. horse   12. Mars   13. Earth   14. month   15. roam   16. shore   17. soar   18. rash
19. hoot   20. shorten   21. reason   22. venom   23. hamster   24. vote   25. storm   26. anthem
27. haven

5   People: Appearance and personality

5·1   1. has   2. is   3. has   4. has   5. has   6. is   7. has   8. is   9. is   10. has   11. is   12. has
13. is   14. is   15. has   16. is (or has *an* average build)   17. has   18. has   19. has   20. has
21. is   22. has   23. has   24. has   25. has   26. has   27. is   28. is   29. has   30. is   31. is
32. has   33. has   34. has   35. has   36. is   37. has   38. is   39. is   40. has   41. has
42. is   43. is   44. has   45. has

5·2   1. mole   2. braces   3. wrinkles   4. scar   5. tattoo   6. stocky   7. bangs   8. freckles   9. bald
10. shaved head   11. average height   12. average build

5·3   1. fitness level   2. facial hair   3. skin blemish   4. height   5. build   6. hair length   7. complexion
8. hairstyle   9. general appearance

5·4   **Describing hairstyles:** hair, blond, dye, older, bald, shoulder-length, shave, curly, braids

Complexion: complexion, light, rosy, ruddy, skin, oily, blemishes, clear, scar

Fitness level: fitness, work, watch, shape, exercise, balanced, fit, spend, activity, out

Language and appearance: issue, acceptable, stereotypes, imply, build, insensitive, neutral

5·5   **Horizontal** (*Across*)

3. Hairstyle   5. Out   6. Pretty   7. Bald   8. Height   11. Ponytail   12. Build
13. Mustache   16. Eyebrows   19. Sideburns   22. Tan   23. Scar   24. Complexion   25. Dye
26. Glasses   27. Average

Vertical (*Down*)

1. Fit   2. Pimples   4. Oily   5. Overweight   7. Blemish   9. Handsome   10. Freckles
12. Braces   13. Mole   14. Appearance   15. Skinny   17. Wrinkles   18. Tattoo   20. Beard
21. Slim   23. Shape

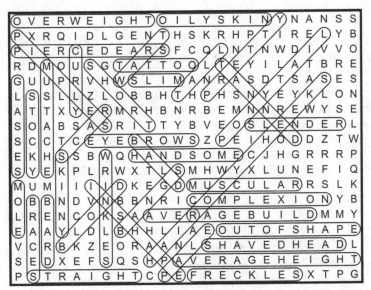

5·7 1. Bossy 2. Athletic 3. Confident 4. Frugal (possibly *stingy*) 5. Punctual 6. Selfish 7. Stubborn 8. Whiney 9. Patient

5·8 1. outgoing 2. brilliant (possibly *witty* or *creative*) 3. obnoxious 4. arrogant 5. articulate 6. considerate 7. reliable 8. heartless

5·9 1. deceitful 2. hardworking 3. narrow-minded (possibly *conservative*) 3. easygoing 4. messy 5. outgoing 6. emotional 7. optimistic

5·10 1. im- 2. dis- 3. un- 4. un- 5. in- 6. dis-

5·11 1. reliable 2. stingy 3. considerate 4. moody 5. impatient 6. polite 7. messy 8. deceitful 9. punctual 10. honest 11. selfish 12. shy 13. rude

Hidden message: A mover and shaker.

5·12

5·13 **Horizontal** (*Across*)

2. Arrogant 5. Punctual 10. Courageous 12. Pessimistic 14. Honest 15. Funny 16. Greedy 19. Lazy 24. Messy 26. Polite 27. Deceitful 28. Stingy 31. Considerate 32. Generous

Vertical (Down)

1. Hardworking 3. Reliable 4. Athletic 6. Thoughtful 7. Positive 8. Bright 9. Outgoing 11. Clever 13. Shy 17. Rude 18. Easygoing 20. Brave 21. Kind 22. Impatient 23. Creative 25. Selfish 29. Neat 30. Wise

5·14 1. couch 2. bird 3. night 4. beaver 5. troublemaker 6. busybody 7. go-getter 8. smart 9. kid 10. cannon 11. daydreamer 12. apple 13. chatterbox 14. camper 15. neck 16. small 17. wolf 18. oddball 19. social

5·15 A leopard cannot change its spots.

6 Travel

6·1 1. luggage 2. carry-on 3. passport 4. visa 5. vacancy 6. cuisine 7. budget 8. postcard 9. destination 10. round-trip 11. voyage 12. board 13. souvenir 14. nightlife 15. monument 16. landmark 17. tourist 18. currency 19. departure 20. flight

6·2 1. people who work in an airport 2. baggage 3. people who work for airlines 4. ticket types 5. gift shop purchases 6. landmarks 7. accommodations 8. tourism-related businesses 9. tourist activities

6·3 **Catching a flight:** flight, arrive, check-in, bags, boarding, security, show, passed, lounge, duty

Traveling on a budget: airline, budget, backpack, package, guesthouses, public, tourists, locals, markets, track

Traveling in style: money, style, star, stress, inclusive, amenities, cruise, swimming, entertainment

Experiencing the local culture: experience, cuisine, exotic, spices, markets, wares, history, festivals, live

6·4 **Horizontal (Across)**

1. Beach 8. Souvenir 9. Holiday 10. Service 12. Landmark 13. Pass 14. Journey 16. Port 17. Train 18. Station 19. Vacation 22. Book 24. Departure 26. Gift 29. Destination 31. Passport 32. Visa 33. Hotel 34. Check 35. Luggage

Vertical (Down)

2. Cuisine 3. Hike 4. Backpack 5. Cruise 6. Round 7. Arrival 9. Honeymoon 11. Resort 15. Airport 16. Pool 20. Tourist 21. One-way 23. Agent 25. Suitcase 27. Flight 28. Motel 30. Show 31. Pack

6·5

6·6 1. book 2. check 3. make 4. order 5. stand 6. clear 7. purchase 8. apply 9. hail 10. pack 11. rent 12. fasten 13. take 14. disturb 15. exchange 16. stow 17. show 18. board 19. request

6·7 **Code breaker:** Cross that bridge when you come to it.

7 Sports

7·1
1. athlete   2. amateur   3. training   4. equipment   5. record   6. league   7. spectator
8. tournament   9. champion   10. match   11. foul   12. sportsmanship   13. trophy
14. stadium   15. court   16. coach   17. judge   18. offense   19. defense   20. score

7·2
1. sports you "do"   2. examples of fouls   3. places where sports are played   4. athletes
5. people who help athletes   6. sports equipment   7. variations of "throw"   8. sporting events
9. sports you "play"

7·3
Training: professional, competitiveness, work, lift, endurance, hone, balanced, injury

Sportsmanship: fair, attitude, rules, breaks, intentionally, decision, arguing, injuring, faking

Tournaments: tournament, champion, elimination, compete, sole, trophy, awarded, ceremonies

Doping: pressure, advertising, enhance, doping, ban, blood, disqualified, titles

7·4
Horizontal (*Across*)
2. Hockey   4. Trophy   6. Pass   8. Court   9. Tie   11. Record   13. Defense   15. Equipment
16. Opponent   17. Whistle   19. Tournament   20. Serve   24. Foul   26. Amateur   27. Defeat
28. Beat   30. Basketball   33. Professional   34. Score

Vertical (*Down*)

1. Soccer   3. Coach   5. Offense   7. Stadium   10. Spectator   12. Champion   14. Athlete
18. Referee   21. Volleyball   22. Goalkeeper   23. Draw   25. Baseball   29. Tennis   31. Block
32. Judge

7·5

7·6
1. ball   2. field   3. ballpark   4. curve   5. course   6. throw   7. league   8. race   9. skate
10. batting   11. ropes   12. count   13. whole   14. bases   15. court   16. bull's-eye   17. holds
18. foul   19. hitter

Code breaker: Slow and steady wins the race.

7·7
1. champion   2. league   3. athlete   4. spectator   5. opponent   6. court   7. amateur   8. referee
9. pass   10. stadium   11. defense   12. record

7·8   **Hidden message:** Nobody likes a sore loser.

8   Weather

8·1   1. calm   2. gusts   3. sleet   4. partly cloudy   5. breeze   6. fog   7. shower   8. frost   9. drizzle   10. overcast   11. flurries   12. gale   13. downpour   14. humid

8·2   **Forms of precipitation:** flurries, drizzle, rain, snow, sleet, shower, hail, blizzard

Cloudy weather: overcast, partly cloudy, fog

Fair weather: clear, calm, sunny, sunshine

Poor visibility weather: fog, blizzard, mist, rain, sleet, hail, flurries, snow

Wind descriptions: windy, gusts, gale, breeze

Low temperatures: chilly, freezing cold, below zero, minus ten

High temperatures: sizzling, scorching, boiling hot

Inclement weather: Any bad or unpleasant weather words.

8·3   1. partly   2. below   3. scattered   4. wind chill   5. inclement   6. gusts   7. ultraviolet   8. boiling   9. freezing   10. minus   11. weather   12. poor

8·4   **Predicting the weather:** forecast, decisions, precipitation, hand, temperatures, outside, meteorologists

The water cycle: force, evaporate, vapor, condenses, frigid, clouds, atmosphere, runoff

Weather forecast 1: humid, high, clear, partly, percent, cool, overcast, up

Weather forecast 2: gusts, severe, gale, batter, advised, abate, drop, lows

Weather forecast 3: forecast, elevations, expected, subside, passes, chains

8·5

8·6   ## Horizontal (*Across*)

5. Chilly   6. Sunshine   8. Drizzle   9. Drought   12. Snow   13. Gusts   15. Partly   17. Breeze   19. Fog   21. Calm   22. Forecast   24. Precipitation   25. Meteorologist   28. Tornado   29. Windy   30. Hurricane   31. Rain

Vertical (*Down*)

1. Cloudy   2. Humidity   3. Flood   4. Sleet   7. Zero   10. Umbrella   11. Hail   12. Snowflake   14. Thermometer   16. Lightning   17. Below   18. Damp   20. Temperature   21. Clear   23. Overcast   26. Shower   27. Cold

8·7   1. shine   2. weather   3. bolt   4. fair weather   5. down   6. rough   7. cloud   8. head   9. wind   10. rainbows   11. storm   12. dogs   13. foggiest   14. breeze   15. lightning   16. rainy   17. tempest   18. sunshine   19. break

8·8   1. Make hay while the sun shines.   2. When it rains, it pours.

8·9   1. flood   2. hurricane   3. meteorologist   4. heatstroke   5. gale force winds   6. barometer
7. tornado   8. cold spell   9. heat wave   10. drought   11. frostbite   12. windchill factor

8·10   **Dangerous weather-related health conditions:** dehydration, hypothermia, frostbite, heatstroke

Extreme temperatures: heat wave, cold spell

Extreme wind conditions: hurricane, gale force winds, tornado

Notices issued when extreme weather is in the forecast: advisory, alert, warning

Tools used by meteorologists: barometer, thermometer, anemometer

Times when there is too little or too much precipitation: drought, flood

8·11   **Extreme winds: the Beaufort scale:** damage, life, advisories, scale, calm, breeze, force, hurricanes

Extreme cold: frigid, dress, consequences, frostbite, amputation, fingers, hypothermia, core

Extreme heat: wave, period, stroke, radiation, colored, perspiration, dehydration, strenuous

Extreme precipitation: precipitation, overflow, bridges, submerge, impassable, drought, wither

8·12   **Horizontal (*Across*)**

5. Spell   6. Precipitation   8. Atmosphere   9. Power   10. Frostbite   11. Thermometer
15. Chill   16. Tornado   18. Drought   21. Hurricane   22. Stroke   23. Blizzard   24. Uprooted

Vertical (*Down*)

1. Crops   2. Wave   3. Temperature   4. Meteorologist   7. Burst   10. Forecast
12. Dehydration   13. Hypothermia   14. Flood   17. Advisory   19. Gale   20. Sunburn

9   Climate

9·1   1. climate   2. arid   3. humid   4. desert   5. fauna   6. flora   7. equator   8. tundra   9. cactus
10. coniferous   11. deciduous   12. prevailing wind   13. monsoon   14. ocean current
15. permafrost   16. taiga   17. rain forest   18. prairie/steppe   19. temperate regions   20. insolation

9·2   1. cold climate biomes   2. grassland biomes   3. factors that affect climate   4. geographical zones
5. living organisms in a region   6. types of trees

9·3   1. tropical   2. rain   3. prevailing   4. annual   5. coniferous   6. flora

9·4   **Climate:** seasonal, temperature, prevailing, fauna, minimal, grasses, support, average, dry

Factors that affect climate: factors, insolation, tropical, affects, continents, milder, mountain, wind, shadow

Deserts and rain forests: Arid, precipitation, flora, adapt, cacti, abundant, sunlight, floor

Polar regions: Arctic, radiation, result, frigid, barren, tundra, taiga, coniferors

9·5   **Horizontal (*Across*)**

1. Coniferous   4. Frigid   6. Tundra   7. Annual   8. Humid   9. Desert   11. Alpine
14. Rain forest   16. Arid   17. Polar   18. Temperature   20. Fauna   21. Monsoon
23. Precipitation   24. Shadow

Vertical (*Down*)

2. Elevation   3. Current   5. Grassland   6. Temperate   10. Equator   12. Permafrost
13. Climate   15. Insolation   17. Prevailing   19. Tropical   20. Flora   21. Mild   22. Taiga

9·6

```
G I L H E T D B V B O C E A N C U R R E N T X C
F X Q K S I J T R O P I C A L R L G S Z V C V A
I G P E R M A F R O S T P A K R I I G D Z M U K
G G R A I N S H A D O W N I K L C Q M X Y N R O
R A I N F O R E S T D N H B X S O P R A I R I E
I N S O L A T I O N A W F Q M Y N T D B T R Q A
J T E Q U A T O R V R J A S W E T L A N D E U K
J A R N T J Q B A F N F U C O R I F B N D O C E
T I T O M O N S O O N O N D A D N C J A L L H X
G G R A S S L A N D R V A L A E E A N G W V C E
A A H U M I D I E A I O R U R N C U W J C T N
L E X Q V S B Z F S B P D A Z A T T I E Y A W E
P L F S H V N I R E N N Q M G R A U J D R I E P
I P L I S O N D Z R U E F T S C L S M E U Y S Z
N P O D X O I F E T W P A S S T E P P E D O Y O
E P R E C I P I T A T I O N W I B M X B M V U U
V U A X N C S R A I N F A L L C E L G K U K G S
V P R E V A I L I N G W I N D T C O A S T A L M
```

10 Clothing and fashion

10·1 1. trend 2. mend 3. vest 4. hoodie 5. overalls 6. tailor 7. suit 8. model 9. secondhand
10. cobbler 11. garment 12. blouse 13. dye 14. mannequin 15. pajamas 16. fashion designer

10·2 1. women's apparel 2. beachwear 3. protective wear 4. formal wear 5. casual
wear 6. eyewear 7. undergarments 8. footwear 9. winter clothes

10·3 **Color/color adjective:** dark, bright, neon, khaki, pastel, turquoise, beige, lavender, navy, light

Pattern: polka dot, checked, animal print, plain/solid, striped, floral print, paisley, argyle, tweed

Material: wool, leather, silk, nylon, polyester, rubber, denim, cotton, suede

Fit/style/occasion: tight, baggy, retro, long-sleeved, formal, casual, turtleneck, loose, sleeveless, short-sleeved, traditional

10·4 1. places where fashion is displayed 2. synonyms for clothes 3. compliments about clothes
4. people working in the fashion industry 5. cosmetics/makeup 6. ways to change clothes
7. fashion accessories 8. things used to keep clothes in place 9. synonyms for fashionable

10·5 **Fashion trends:** fashion, in, stylish, conscious, trend, fads, novelty, out, retro

Fashion show: show, models, designs, photographers, runway, magazine

Shopping for clothes: window, mannequins, latest, outfit, catches, try, dressing

Choosing the right clothes: fits, tight, uncomfortable, looks, match, suit

Shopping on a budget: afford, into, secondhand, prices, online, steep, sale

10·6

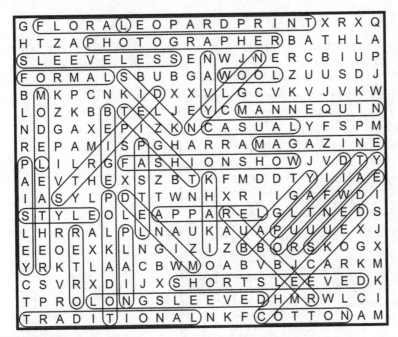

10·7 Horizontal (*Across*)

1. Pajamas   7. Sandals   9. Dress   10. Overalls   12. Plain   13. Scarf   14. Formal
15. Hat   17. High   18. Model   20. Needle   22. Tailor   23. Bikini   24. Dye   28. Shirt   30. Try
31. Socks   33. Shoes   34. Gloves   36. Stylish   37. Wool

Vertical (*Down*)

1. Pants   2. Jeans   3. Striped   4. Good   5. Polka   6. Boots   7. Sweater   8. Secondhand
11. Leather   12. Plaid   14. Fashion   16. Tie   18. Match   19. Loose   21. Denim   23. Baggy
25. Blouse   26. Silk   27. Fits   28. Shorts   29. Floral   30. Tight   32. Suit   35. Sew

11   The arts: Performing and visual

11·1   1. actor   2. comedian   3. composer   4. mime   5. magician   6. costumes   7. audience
8. applause   9. script   10. musical   11. spontaneous   12. spotlight   13. theater   14. stage
15. prop/scenery/set   16. stand-up   17. comedy   18. tragedy   19. illusion   20. ballet   21. score
22. gesture   23. choreography

11·2   1. types of plays   2. performing artists   3. things done at a rehearsal   4. things performers wear
5. documents used by performers   6. people who direct performers

11·3   **The performing arts:** opera, performing, bodies, ballerinas, stand-up, magic, comedian, jokes, illusions

Taking part in a musical: putting, try, audition, talent, part, rehearsal, cast, memorize, audience

The theater: theater, comedies, tragedies, stage, actors, costumes, makeup, props, set

Choreography: choreography, sequences, dance, fashion, cheerleading, gymnastics, synchronized, skating, fight

11·4   **Horizontal (*Across*)**

1. Costume   3. Perform   5. Musician   8. Audition   9. Illusion   13. Choreography
14. Choir   15. Makeup   19. Tragedy   21. Audience   23. Applause   28. Composer   29. Lines
30. Gesture

Vertical (*Down*)

1. Comedian 2. Musical 4. Magician 5. Mime 6. Conductor 7. Spotlight 10. Stage
11. Orchestra 12. Prop 13. Comedy 16. Script 17. Rehearsal 18. Ballet 20. Dialogue
22. Concert 24. Clown 25. Score 26. Band 27. Mask

11·5

```
W H A L A E P R L N R S E H M S P O T L I G H T
Y B H K H O J F O Y O H Q C O S T U M E C L X D
V R E D R J K I D E C F Z A K M A K C L M U S T
U H V P S P T E W B L V Q S M A U E Y G M U E R
Z L D E J I M O S I O G A X B A L S G L V R S C
E H T N D O T H K A W M J B P F K U I T F V U Y
X H R U C M O E R K N K D Y A O R E F C P R M E
C O A M G E S T U R E Q D I A L O G U E I M Y O
O K G P P M S N L P U T L S D N L D O P Q A M F
M P E I R E H E A R S A L Z X S P E P Y J R N T
P E D R H A R A J U C I B X W Y J W T S A Y I W
O R Y C F Y P N T I D L U G C O N D U C T O R W
S F R L M P I P S Y P I D G H I L L U S I O N S
E O U S J I U C O N C E R T P K I Q U I A O F
R R B A C R M A G I C I A N H K Z N T S Z N G O
X M A R C O D E I Q U O T N C O M E D I A N V D
W H N S C H R S T G C H O I R E W S T A G E D J
C Q D C H O R E O G R A P H Y A P P L A U S E J
```

11·6 1. horn 2. piper 3. song 4. mirrors 5. curtain 6. fiddle 7. break 8. music 9. magic
10. act 11. show 12. limelight 13. laughs 14. scenes 15. circuses 16. tune 17. stage
18. tango 19. clown

11·7 1. Practice makes perfect. 2. The show must go on.

11·8 1. illustrate/sketch 2. carve/etch 3. masterpiece 4. visual 5. exhibit/exhibition 6. portfolio
7. background 8. foreground 9. mural 10. mosaic 11. point of view 12. perspective drawing
13. realistic 14. abstract 15. depict/portray 16. sculpture 17. texture 18. shading
19. creativity/originality 20. hues 21. vivid 22. portrait

11·9 1. works of art 2. visual artists 3. methods of creating art 4. places to view art
5. elements of an artwork 6. drawings

11·10 **The visual arts:** creation, sculpture, experience, appreciation, provocative, statement, practical, furniture

Types of visual arts: visual, canvas, sculpting, metal, murals, mosaics, popularity, designers

Realism: resembles, realistic, Renaissance, technique, works, posterity, perspective, converge, depth

Abstract art: Invention, realism, experimenting, abstract, view, emotions, physical, shapes

11·11 ## Horizontal (*Across*)

1. Foreground 5. Carve 6. Abstract 9. Mural 11. Painter 13. Illustrate
14. Perspective 15. Visual 16. Sketch 21. Depict 23. Masterpiece 24. Image 26. Mosaic
27. Original

Vertical (*Down*)

2. Graffiti 3. Resemble 4. Sculpture 7. Ceramics 8. Point 10. Realistic 12. Canvas
17. Exhibition 18. Hue 19. Background 20. Creativity 22. Portfolio 23. Museum 25. Artist

11·12

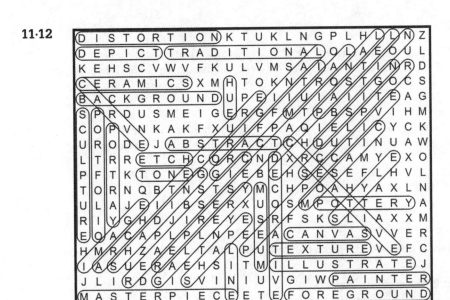

11·13 1. visual   2. realistic   3. abstract   4. illustrate   5. image   6. carve   7. depict   8. masterpiece
9. original   10. mural   11. hues

Hidden Message: In the eye of the beholder.

12   Jobs and occupations

12·1 1. caterer   2. security guard   3. real estate agent   4. architect   5. inspector   6. civil servant
7. trainer   8. guidance counselor   9. social worker   10. janitor   11. electrician   12. editor
13. physician   14. courier   15. journalist   16. mechanic   17. telemarketer   18. consultant

12·2 1. construction/trades   2. health care   3. hospitality   4. information technology   5. agriculture
6. tourism   7. media   8. resource extraction   9. education

12·3

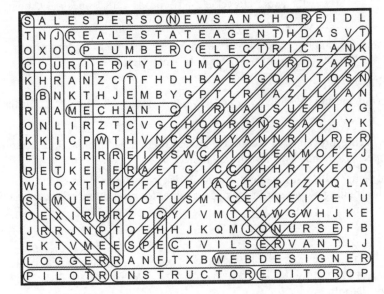

1. Social   5. Rancher   7. Guide   9. Detective   10. Physician   12. Dentist   14. Janitor   15. Plumber   20. Inspector   21. Real estate   22. Caterer   24. Construction   25. Telemarketer

Vertical (*Down*)

1. Security   2. Chef   3. Logger   4. Agent   6. Architect   8. Mechanic   10. Pilot   11. Consultant   13. Teller   14. Journalist   16. Electrician   17. Miner   18. Forecaster   19. Farmer   22. Courier   23. Civil

13   Work life

13·1 **Voluntary:** leave your job, quit your job, resign, retire

Involuntary: be asked to leave, be dismissed, be given notice, be made redundant, get fired, get canned/sacked, get laid off

Poor work performance: get fired, get canned/sacked

Reasons beyond your control: be made redundant, get laid off

13·2 1. dead-end   2. cover   3. job   4. computer   5. team   6. prospective   7. want   8. win-win   9. sick   10. application   11. dental   12. pleasant

13·3 1. for   2. in/out   3. from   4. for   5. from   6. in   7. for   8. for   9. in

13·4 **Deciding to get a job:** looking, graduated, loans, dissatisfied, challenge, salary, benefits, laid, fired

Searching for jobs: listings, classified, bulletin, centers, headhunter, Internet, resume, mouth, networking

Finding the right job: paying, compensation, satisfaction, lower, health, plan, free, long, little

Applying for and accepting a job: apply, application, resume, cover, candidate, interview, offer, accept, contract

13·5 1. box   2. buck   3. jump   4. sleeves   5. foot   6. scratch   7. fence   8. mind   9. wing   10. day   11. feet   12. leg   13. head   14. eyes   15. ears   16. clock   17. heads   18. ropes   19. boat

13·6 1. Bite off more than you can chew.   2. Have a lot on your plate.

13·7 1. résumé   2. salary   3. wage   4. apply   5. creative   6. raise   7. contract   8. promotion   9. pension   10. employer   11. benefit   12. skill   13. tip   14. interview

Hidden message: Pull a few strings.

13·8 1. pension   2. salary   3. remuneration (possibly *salary* or *wage*)   4. wage   5. tip   6. commissions

13·9 Answers will vary.

Qualifications might include: license, proven track record, volunteer experience, diploma, skills, training, certificate, degree, education, specialized knowledge, work experience.

Benefits might include: dental plan, health insurance/medical plan, sick leave, tips, commissions, job satisfaction, remuneration, skills, training, wage, education, opportunities for promotion, salary, specialized knowledge, vacation, work experience.

13·10 **Horizontal** (*Across*)

1. High   3. Laid   4. Box   6. Hire   9. Cover   10. Wage   11. Ethic   14. Retire   15. Qualifications   18. Employer   22. Promotion   23. People   24. Works   25. Skills   27. Resume   28. Dental   29. Deadlines

Vertical (Down)

1. Health 2. Hardworking 3. Leave 4. Benefits 5. Experience 7. Occupation
8. Fired 12. Salary 13. Raise 16. Interview 17. Degree 19. Contract 20. Classifieds
21. Apply 22. Pressure 23. Pension 26. Team

13·11 **Quitting a dead-end job:** dissatisfied, position, raise, dead-end, dust, prospective, interview, anticipate

Reasons for changing jobs: reasons, negative, mouth, problems, team, positive, challenging, advancement

Why work here? employers, research, skills, goals, win-win, stick, costly, long-term

Your strengths and weaknesses: Strengths, relevant, pressure, box, ethic, deadlines, honest

13·12

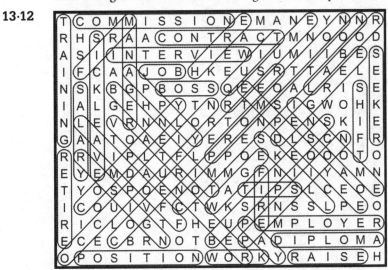

13·13 **Proverb 1:** Many hands make light work.

Proverb 2: Too many cooks spoil the broth.

13·4 1. brown 2. orbit 3. enter 4. town 5. iron 6. tree 7. twin 8. never 9. invite 10. rob
11. vote 12. toe 13. wire 14. went 15. review 16. winter 17. even 18. note 19. verb
20. event 21. win 22. nerve 23. tire 24. oven 25. bone 26. vow 27. teen 28. new

14 Parts of the body

14·1 1. earlobe 2. joint 3. sole 4. fist 5. nostrils 6. forehead 7. wrist 8. ankle 9. heel
10. pinky 11. thigh 12. waist 13. cheek 14. temple 15. index 16. jaw 17. chin
18. eyelashes 19. eyebrows 20. groin 21. palm 22. calf

14·2 **Parts of your face:** cheek, chin, earlobe, ears, eyebrows, eyelashes, eyelid, eyes, forehead, lips, nose, nostrils, temple

Joint locations: ankle, elbow, hip, knee, knuckles, wrist, shoulder

Parts of a leg: calf, thigh, shin, ankle, knee, hip, foot

Fingers: index, thumb, pinky, ring, middle

Parts of a foot: sole, toes, ankle, heel

14·3 **Your hands:** grasping, opposable, tools, receptors, temperature, gesturing, wave, thumbs, offensive

Your face: face, chin, cheeks, communication, feel, smile, frown, eyebrows, question, roll

Your legs: crawl, erect, advantage, feet, sole, ankle, knee, thigh, calf, shin

Abdomen and chest: organs, abdomen, intestines, chest, lungs, shoulders, groin, belly, spine

Horizontal (*Across*)

2. Ankle   5. Calf   9. Ears   11. Abdomen   12. Thigh   14. Temple   15. Heel   16. Eyelashes
18. Finger   21. Shin   22. Wrist   23. Spine   24. Eyes   25. Palm   26. Earlobe   27. Jaw
28. Knee

Vertical (*Down*)

1. Hand   3. Eyebrows   4. Thumb   5. Cheek   6. Fist   7. Chin   8. Knuckles   10. Shoulder
13. Chest   17. Eyelid   19. Nostril   20. Forehead   23. Sole   24. Elbow   25. Pinky

14·5

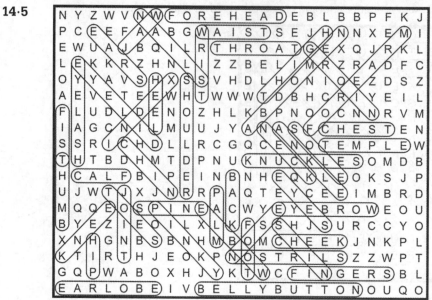

14·6   1. nerves   2. lungs   3. hearts   4. brain   5. blink   6. elbow   7. back   8. heel   9. blood
10. tongue   11. ears   12. mouth   13. skeleton   14. hairs   15. neck   16. breathe   17. hands
18. skin   19. arm

14·7   1. All brawn and no brain.   2. Cost an arm and a leg.

15   Common ailments

15·1   1. toothache   2. indigestion   3. stomachache   4. rash   5. allergies   6. burn   7. cut
8. cough   9. bump   10. sprained ankle   11. blister   12. vomiting   13. blurred vision
14. dizziness   15. itchiness   16. fever   17. diarrhea   18. constipation   19. broken bone
20. bruise

15·2   Answers will vary.

Injuries might include: bite/sting, black eye, broken bone, bruise, bump, burn, cut, scrape/scratch, sprained ankle.

Illnesses might include: allergies, common cold, congestion, constipation, diarrhea, fever, flu, headache/migraine, heartburn/indigestion, insomnia, sore throat, stomachache, toothache.

15·3   **Allergies:** suffer, spring, allergies, pollen, itchy, breathing, immune, allergens, trigger

The common cold: runny, congestion, sore, symptoms, viral, caught, winter, contagious, avoid, hands

Injuries versus illnesses: confuse, infections, wrong, flu, sprained, stubbed, sick, hurt

Skin ailments: skin, ailments, rash, irritants, itchy, relieve, burns, sunburns, cuts

Horizontal (*Across*)

2. Flu   4. Black   6. Ache   7. Take   8. Vomit   9. Drink   11. Runny   12. Burn
13. Shot   15. Symptom   17. Vision   20. Insomnia   23. Sprained   26. Illness   27. Headache
28. Allergy

Vertical (*Down*)

1. Broken   2. Fever   3. Get   5. Common   10. Injury   11. Rash   12. Bump
14. Toothache   15. Sore   16. Medicine   18. Sting   19. Bruise   21. See   22. Itchy   24. Recover
25. Dizzy

15·5

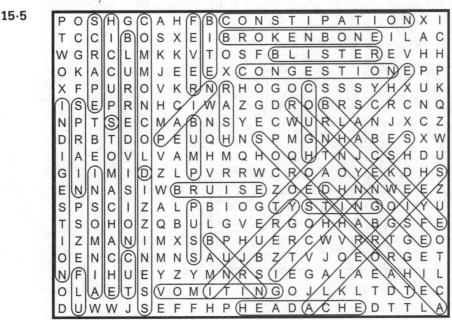

15·6   1. weather   2. feet   3. prescription   4. head   5. knife   6. nerves   7. checkup   8. temperature
9. splitting   10. mend   11. road   12. health   13. fiddle   14. grave   15. hay   16. balanced
17. plenty   18. rest   19. regular

15·7   An apple a day keeps the doctor away.

16   Government and citizenship

16·1   1. legislative   2. executive   3. judicial   4. federal/national   5. state/provincial   6. municipal
7. president   8. governor   9. mayor   10. democracy   11. monarchy   12. dictatorship
13. civil rights   14. responsibilities   15. Supreme Court   16. Constitution   17. amendment
18. checks and balances   19. bill   20. representative

16·2   1. taxes levied by government   2. branches of government   3. government services
4. heads of government   5. citizen responsibilities   6. systems of government

16·3   **Citizen rights and obligations:** member, rights, discriminated, race, beliefs, express, responsibilities, taxes, obey

Government services: services, maintained, emergency, provide, good, firefighters, collect, income

The legislative branch: branches, legislative, lawmakers, bill, Congress, Parliament, vote, passes

The executive and judicial branches: executive, enforce, armed, president, judicial, broken, resolving, appeal, Supreme

Horizontal (*Across*)

1. Democracy   6. Court   8. Constitution   9. Mayor   11. Government   15. Supreme
17. Judicial   18. Executive   21. Taxes   22. Responsibilities   25. President   26. Law

Vertical (*Down*)

2. Monarchy   3. Checks   4. Vote   5. Rights   6. Citizen   7. Assembly   10. Representative
12. Dictatorship   13. Legislative   14. Election   16. Services   19. Municipal   20. Enforce
23. Obey   24. Bill

16·5

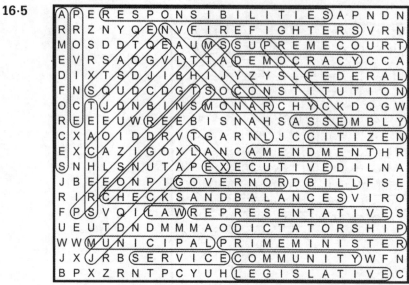

16·6   1. citizen   2. court   3. constitution   4. rights   5. judge   6. municipal   7. mayor   8. law
9. service   10. legislative   11. executive   12. judicial

Checks and Balances

17   Geography

17·1   1. latitude   2. longitude   3. contour lines   4. border   5. prime meridian   6. equator
7. Tropic of Cancer   8. Tropic of Capricorn   9. Arctic Circle   10. Antarctic Circle
11. compass rose   12. map key   13. scale   14. the poles   15. terrain   16. atlas   17. globe
18. political map   19. topographical   20. physical

17·2   1. names of continents   2. types of maps   3. names of oceans   4. things used to decipher a map
5. lines of latitude   6. ways to indicate elevation

17·3   1. topographical   2. tropic   3. prime   4. arctic   5. contour   6. sea level

17·4   **Types of maps:** borders, political, features, ranges, physical, topographical, lines, level

Lines on map: Location, longitude, prime, latitude, equator, Tropic, Circle, Pole, south, coordinates

Continents and oceans: continents, depends, combined, Eurasia, South, oceans, Pacific, Arctic, Antarctica

Deciphering a map: Decipher, compass, scale, reality, legend, symbols, circle, capital

17·5   **Horizontal** (*Across*)

2. Political   5. Coast   6. Globe   8. Tropic   10. Continent   12. Capital   13. Legend   15. Circle
17. Topographical   19. Coordinates   21. Atlas   22. Hemisphere   24. Key   25. Latitude   27. Rose

Vertical (*Down*)

1. Contour   3. Location   4. Longitude   7. Equator   9. Prime   11. Elevation   14. Geography
16. Scale   17. Terrain   18. Ocean   20. Border   23. Pole   26. Date

```
D L K Q T N O R T H P O L E Y I P C D W C C Q U
M R U M Q R S P R I M E M E R I D I A N N E C H
G L O B E E O C S D S X E D L T Z C J R R S G R
T I G Q Q B O P A S C O M P A S S R O S E U E J
O S Y B Z B D U I L D V U J P Y Q C W T I A C E
P C N N T V U W A C E S N N H H I L A W Y V L U
O O C M A P K E Y T O F O P L R Y N C N C C V U
G N I O V O K O Y C O F A V P O I S O R R W Q B
R T C T N M R R V S A R C A H D N I I A G I S
A O T S Y T Z A V G P C A R E T G C C U M O B
P U H U L N I L C O C F I O N A M C I K A Q G M
H R Z H U M T N E A O T O T V C I T T S L R G
I L Q O C A M G E C A C W E A T E N S W U M H U
C I C A I M D O X N S P L E C L T R J P V D F P
A N W Q T P U P C E T E R R A I N P F Q H D E I
L E X Y Y B O R D E R L A T I T U D E E U E M M
G S I R M R I H B Z A V J C N Z N O P L K N R Z
P O L I T I C A L Q N N Y S O U T H P O L E Z E
```

17·7 1. peninsula 2. island 3. lake 4. atoll 5. volcano 6. delta 7. landform 8. archipelago 9. mountain range 10. slope 11. cliff 12. plain 13. plateau 14. reef 15. glacier 16. estuary 17. tributary 18. river basin

17·8 **Flowing bodies of freshwater:** stream, creek, river

Bodies of water surrounded by land on three sides: cove, bay, gulf

Places where land meets water: beach, shore, coast

Narrow bodies of water that separate two landmasses: straight, channel

Saltwater bodies that extend deep into the land: fjord, inlet

The top of a mountain: summit, peak, apex

17·9 **River basins:** flows, tributary, basin, delta, sedimentation, mouth, estuary, tide

Highlands: formed, crust, ranges, peak, summit, slope, cliff, similar, plateau

Where land meets sea: shore, peninsula, gulf, bay, surrounded, archipelago, eruptions, atolls

Land sculpted by ice: age, temperature, glaciers, eroded, fjords, boulders, level, connected

17·10 ## Horizontal (*Across*)

3. Delta 4. Estuary 7. Bay 9. Reef 10. Slope 13. Island 14. Waterfall 17. Canyon 18. Plateau 19. Atoll 20. Archipelago 23. Cave

Vertical (*Down*)

1. Valley 2. Coast 5. Range 6. Straight 7. Basin 8. Tributary 11. Peninsula 12. Stream 15. Landform 16. Glacier 18. Peak 21. Plain 22. Lake 23. Cliff

17·11

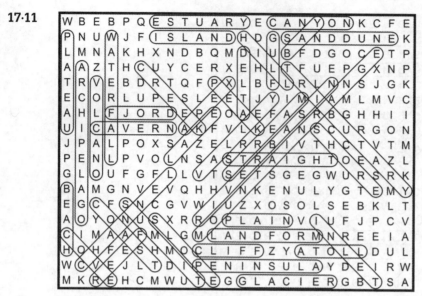

```
W B E B P Q E S T U A R Y E C A N Y O N K C F E
P N U W J F I S L A N D H D G S A N D D U N E K
L M N A K H X N D B Q M D I U B F D G O C E T P
A A Z T H C U Y C E R X E H L T F U E P G X N P
T R V E B D R T Q F P X L B F U R L N N S J G K
E C O R L U P E S L E E T J Y I M I A M L M V C
A H L F J O R D E P E O A E F A S R B G H H I I
U I C A V E R N A K F V L K E A N S C U R G O N
J P A L P O X S A Z L R R B I V T H C T V T M
P E N L P V O L N S A S T R A I G H T O E A Z L
G L O U F G F L L V T S E T S G E G W U R S R K
B A M G N V E V Q H H V N K E N U L Y G T E M Y
E G C F S N C G V W I U Z X O S O L S E B K L T
A O Y O N U S X R R O P L A I N V I U F J P C V
C I M A A F M L G M L A N D F O R M N R E E I A
H O H F E S H M O C L I F F Z Y A T O L L D U L
W C V E J L T D I P E N I N S U L A Y D E I R W
M K R E H C M W U T E G G L A C I E R G B T S A
```

17·12   1. archipelago   2. peninsula   3. tributary   4. valley   5. glacier   6. delta   7. slope   8. cliff   9. canyon   10. island   11. plain   12. plateau

The tip of the iceberg.

17·13   1. echo   2. chore   3. replica   4. girl   5. April   6. glacier   7. cape   8. coal   9. gear   10. peach   11. choir   12. leap   13. pearl   14. liar   15. carol   16. oracle   17. peril   18. rice   19. hair   20. hero   21. cheap   22. oar   23. core   24. gale   25. chirp   26. race   27. poach   28. cargo

18   Disasters

18·1   1. epidemic   2. earthquake   3. drought   4. power outage   5. civil war   6. famine   7. volcanic eruption   8. avalanche   9. war   10. flood   11. heat wave   12. tsunami   13. wildfire   14. blizzard   15. riot   16. landslide

18·2   Answers will vary.

Natural disasters might include: avalanche, earthquake, heat wave, tornado, typhoon, blizzard, epidemic, hurricane, volcanic eruption, cyclone, famine, wildfire, drought, flood, landslide, tsunami.

Human-caused disasters might include: collapsed bridge, mine explosion, power outage, collapsed building, nuclear meltdown, riot, toxic contamination, building fire, gas leak, oil spill, shipwreck, train derailment, wildfire, civil war, plane crash, terrorist attack, war.

18·3   1. nuclear meltdown   2. flood   3. volcanic eruption   4. avalanche   5. shipwreck   6. power outage   7. epidemic   8. oil spill

18·4   **Horizontal (*Across*)**

1. Flood   5. Survivor   6. Coast guard   8. Emergency   12. Shipwreck   14. Riot   15. Avalanche   21. Tornado   22. War   23. Civil   25. Contamination   26. Wave

Vertical (*Down*)

1. Famine   2. Outage   3. Drought   4. Wildfire   7. Tsunami   9. Eruption   10. Blizzard   11. Meltdown   13. Crash   16. Ambulance   17. Earthquake   18. Hurricane   19. Landslide   20. Hospital   23. Change   24. Spill

18·5 **Drought:** precipitation, consequences, crops, livestock, famine, migrate, erosion

Flood: flood, heavy, sandbags, river, life, damage, rescuers, submerged, bridges

Hurricanes: ocean, evacuate, winds, rains, windows, property, typhoons, cyclones

Volcanoes: eruptions, molten, catastrophic, lava, ash, toxic

Earthquakes: lethal, collapse, rubble, pipes, casualties, lack, sewer, epidemic

18·6 1. donate to charity   2. refugees   3. an aid worker (other answers possible)   4. clear roads   5. evacuate people   6. rescue worker (other answers possible)   7. survivors   8. treat the injured   9. rebuild   10. dig through rubble

18·7 **People involved in disasters:** aid worker, casualty, rescue worker, National Guard, refugees, firefighters, survivors, coast guard, victim

Things people do to help: clean up, clear roads, contact loved ones, deliver aid, dig through rubble, donate to charity, evacuate people, rebuild, remove debris, rescue survivors, search for survivors, treat the injured, volunteer to help

Emergency situations: calamity, catastrophe, disaster, crash, wreck

18·8 1. coast guard   2. refugees   3. casualty/survivor   4. aid worker   5. firefighter

18·9 1. sole   2. natural   3. volcanic   4. severe   5. collapsed   6. heat   7. first   8. toxic   9. loss   10. nuclear   11. death   12. property

18·10

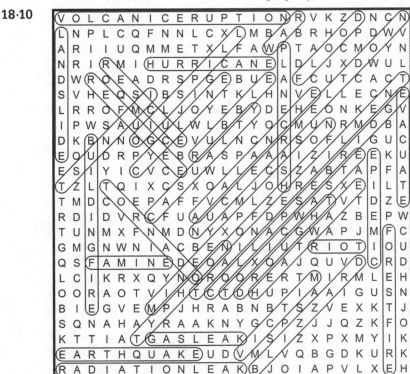

18·11 1. pool   2. trap   3. iron   4. acorn   5. clone   6. train   7. onion   8. arctic   9. coal   10. captive   11. tunnel   12. utopia   13. coupon   14. noon   15. alien   16. ancient   17. coin   18. convince   19. lunatic   20. polite   21. icicle   22. rain   23. pirate   24. critic   25. ocean   26. concur   27. centaur   28. location